CRITICAL THINKING MADE EASY

A STEP-BY-STEP GUIDE TO SHARPEN YOUR LOGICAL AND STRATEGIC INTELLIGENCE WITHOUT CLASSES, COURSES, OR DRAMATICALLY CHANGING YOUR SCHEDULE

OVER THE HORIZON PRESS

© **Copyright Over The Horizon Press 2024 - All rights reserved.**

The content within this book may not be reproduced, duplicated or transmitted without direct written permission from the author or the publisher.

Under no circumstances will any blame or legal responsibility be held against the publisher, or author, for any damages, reparation, or monetary loss due to the information contained within this book. Either directly or indirectly. You are responsible for your own choices, actions, and results.

Legal Notice:

This book is copyright protected. This book is only for personal use. You cannot amend, distribute, sell, use, quote or paraphrase any part, of the content within this book, without the consent of the author or publisher.

Disclaimer Notice:

Please note the information contained within this document is for educational and entertainment purposes only. All effort has been expended to present accurate, up-to-date, and reliable, complete information. No warranties of any kind are declared or implied. Readers acknowledge that the author is not engaging in the rendering of legal, financial, medical or professional advice. The content within this book has been derived from various sources. Please consult a licensed professional before attempting any techniques outlined in this book.

By reading this document, the reader agrees that under no circumstances is the author responsible for any losses, direct or indirect, which are incurred as a result of the use of the information contained within this document, including, but not limited to, — errors, omissions, or inaccuracies.

CONTENTS

Introduction — 5

1. Understanding Critical Thinking — 9
2. Tools for Thought — 27
3. Rational Thinking In The Digital Age — 47
4. Problem Solving in Personal Decisions — 61
5. Wisdom In The Workplace — 79
6. Practical Exercises for Everyday Thought — 103
7. Overcoming Obstacles to Critical Thinking — 119
8. Advanced Strategies: Making Decisions That Make Sense — 135
9. Promoting Insightful Thinking in Communities — 153
10. The Future of Critical Thinking — 169

Conclusion — 189
References — 193

INTRODUCTION

Have you ever watched a simple misunderstanding on social media spiral out of control? A comment taken out of context, a joke that lands poorly, or a fact that's not quite a fact are daily digital dilemmas indicating a critical gap in our collective skill set: critical thinking. It's a scene all too familiar, underscoring the pivotal role that critical thinking—or the lack thereof—plays in our everyday lives.

My journey into the world of critical thinking wasn't born out of an academic fascination or a desire to write yet another textbook on the subject. It stemmed from a simple yet profound realization. In our fast-paced, information-overloaded world, the ability to sift through the noise, analyze arguments, and make well-informed decisions is not just nice to have but rather a necessity. This book is my attempt to break down the barriers that have made critical thinking seem inaccessible to so many. It's an invitation to every adult, regardless of age, profession, or educational background, to enhance their logical and strategic intelligence in a way that fits into their everyday lives.

The purpose of "Critical Thinking Made Easy" is to strip away the complexity and academia surrounding the concept of critical thinking. This book is designed to be your guide, making it straightforward for anyone to bolster their cognitive skills. You won't have to enroll in classes, attend any expensive workshops, or drastically change your daily routine. The key steps to developing critical thinking are simple and easy to follow.

This book was designed to take simple, gradual steps to guide you through the core elements of critical thinking before showing you how to use it in your everyday life—at home, in the office, or navigating the digital world. Each chapter will guide you with practical exercises, real-life examples, and straightforward advice to ensure not only a deeper understanding of critical thinking but also the ability to apply these skills in daily situations.

What sets this book apart is its commitment to clarity and practicality. You won't find complicated, academic wording or vague thoughts. Instead, the material in this book is designed to give you an abundance of actionable insights and simple yet effective exercises designed to engage your mind and sharpen your critical thinking skills.

By following along with the steps in this book, you'll be able to make significant strides toward improving your decision-making skills, enhancing your problem-solving capabilities, and fine-tuning your ability to navigate the complexities of the modern world. These skills are invaluable not just for personal fulfillment but are also critical for professional success in an ever-changing landscape.

As we embark on this journey together, remember that the objective is not just to learn about critical thinking but to live it. Regardless of where you're starting from, this book is crafted to help you become a more insightful and strategic thinker by facing your challenges with rationality and confidence.

Now, I invite you to dive into the first chapter with an eager mind and a commitment to transformation. Engage actively with the exercises, reflect on your progress, and watch as the world opens up in ways you never imagined. Let's begin this journey towards unlocking your full potential as a critical thinker.

CHAPTER 1
UNDERSTANDING CRITICAL THINKING

Have you ever found yourself at the receiving end of a sales pitch that sounds too good to be true? Or perhaps you've been part of a work meeting where ideas were thrown around, but none seemed to stick? These scenarios aren't just tests of patience; they're golden opportunities to apply critical thinking. Once honed, it's a skill that can radically transform how you perceive, interact with, and respond to the world around you. This chapter is your starting block, your foundational guide to understanding what critical thinking really entails and why it's so crucial, especially in today's fast-paced, information-heavy environment.

1.1 DEFINING CRITICAL THINKING IN THE MODERN WORLD

Definition and Scope:

Critical thinking is often tossed around as a buzzword in job descriptions and educational objectives. Still, its core is profoundly simple and universally applicable. It involves analyzing a situation and evaluating for a reasonable result. It's not about thinking more or thinking harder; it's about approaching thinking differently. You break down information. You build it up into coherent ideas. You weigh them against each other. Then, you draw your conclusions not from gut feelings or guesswork but from reasoned and deliberate consideration.

Relevance Today:

We live in an era where information is abundant and easy to access. However, misinformation is running more rampant than ever. The ability to dissect this information, to distinguish between what's credible and what's not, has never been more **critical**. Every day, whether it's in the news we read, the posts we scroll through on social media, or the conversations we have, there's a constant need to evaluate the accuracy and integrity of the information presented to us. Developing your critical thinking skills empowers you to do just that, making navigating the landscape of modern misinformation easier, ensuring you're not easily swayed by falsehoods or manipulations. It acts as a filter, a necessary tool to navigate the complexities of modern information landscapes, ensuring you're not swayed by falsehoods or manipulations.

Skills Involved:

Critical thinking only involves a few key skills: analysis, evaluation, inference, and explanation.

- **Analysis** is about breaking down complex information into understandable parts.
- **Evaluation** involves assessing the credibility and significance of information.
- **Inference** is about drawing reasonable conclusions from the information at hand.
- **Explanation** is about justifying your reasoning.

Mastering these skills means approaching any situation, problem, or decision with a clear, structured thought process that leads to better outcomes.

Misconceptions:

There's a common misconception that critical thinking is just a natural skill—either you have it or you don't. This is far from the truth. Like any other skill, critical thinking can be learned, practiced, and improved. Another widespread misunderstanding is that critical thinking is purely negative—always about critiquing or finding faults. On the contrary, critical thinking is constructive; it's about building robust arguments, finding innovative solutions, and fostering creative thoughts. It's not about being argumentative; it's about being informed and thoughtful.

Visual Element: Critical Thinking Skills Chart

To help encapsulate the skills involved in critical thinking, below is a simple chart that breaks down each skill with a brief description and an example:

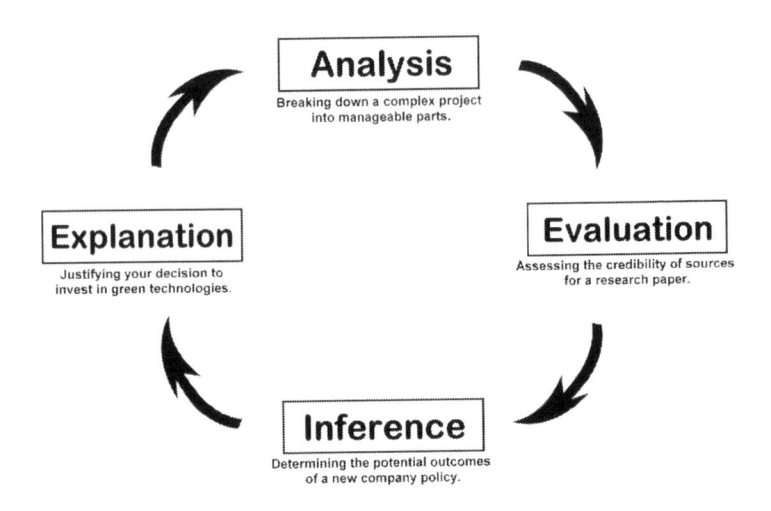

Analysis
Breaking down a complex project into manageable parts.

Evaluation
Assessing the credibility of sources for a research paper.

Inference
Determining the potential outcomes of a new company policy.

Explanation
Justifying your decision to invest in green technologies.

This chart serves as a quick reference to help you understand and recall the essential skills as you progress through more complex scenarios and exercises in the coming chapters. Remember, these skills are your tools for cutting through the noise of everyday information and making decisions that are not just good but justified and reasonable.

1.2 THE HISTORY OF CRITICAL THOUGHT AND ITS EVOLUTION

The roots of critical thinking are deeply entrenched in the rich soil of ancient philosophy, where the likes of Socrates, Plato, and Aristotle planted the earliest seeds of inquiry and rational thought. With his relentless questioning, Socrates claimed that an unexamined life was not worth living. His dialectic method, known as the Socratic Method, involved asking a series of probing questions to challenge assumptions and encourage deeper understanding. Plato, Socrates' most famous student, expanded on these ideas and emphasized the importance of reasoning in his allegory of the cave, which portrays how education moves the soul toward light and truth. Aristotle, Plato's student, further developed the foundations of logical reasoning, creating systematic processes for logical argumentation that are still studied today.

As centuries passed, the flame of critical thought was carried through the darkness of the Middle Ages by the scholars of the Renaissance, who rekindled the ancient Greek interest in humanism and empirical evidence. This period saw figures like Leonardo da Vinci and Galileo Galilei, who combined art and science to challenge established norms and enhance human understanding of the natural world. The Renaissance set the stage for the Enlightenment, a pivotal era that championed reason as the primary source of authority and legitimacy. Philosophers like John Locke, who argued that knowledge comes from experience and reason, and Immanuel Kant, who famously critiqued pure reason to explore the limits and capabilities of human understanding, were instrumental in pushing the boundaries of critical thinking during this period.

The contributions of these key figures have had a profound and lasting impact on the development of critical thinking. René Descartes, another monumental figure, introduced a method of doubt and questioning that remains a hallmark of critical inquiry. His famous declaration, "Cogito, ergo sum" ("I think, therefore I am"), not only underscored the importance of doubt in critical thinking but also highlighted the inherent connection between thinking and existence. These philosophers collectively laid down the intellectual frameworks that challenged the status quo and encouraged a more analytical approach to understanding the world.

The evolution of critical thinking is not just a chronology of great thinkers but also a narrative that reflects its impact on education over time. Initially, education was about memorizing facts and the uncritical acceptance of received wisdom. However, as the concept of critical thinking took root, educational theories began to emphasize its importance. This shift became particularly evident in the 20th century with the emergence of educational reformers like John Dewey, who championed critical thinking as an essential educational goal. Dewey argued that education should not merely be about transferring information but should empower students to think independently and critically, engage with their environments, and solve problems creatively.

Today, the influence of these philosophical and educational shifts is evident in educational curricula worldwide, which increasingly prioritize critical thinking skills. These curricula aim to prepare students not just to consume information but to analyze, question, and create. In a world where information is abundant and misinformation is common, thinking critically is more important than ever. It serves as a crucial tool for navigating the challenges of modern life, from making informed decisions in the voting booth to discerning reliable sources of information in a digital age overflowing with data. The historical evolution of critical thinking, from ancient philosophy to modern education, highlights its enduring relevance and the continued need to nurture this vital skill for current and future generations.

1.3 IDENTIFYING YOUR CURRENT THINKING PATTERNS

Self-awareness is the cornerstone of effective critical thinking. It's about catching yourself in the act—recognizing when your thoughts are running on autopilot and understanding the patterns that dominate your thinking. For instance, consider a typical workday scenario where you might make a snap judgment about a colleague's comment during a meeting. Perhaps you interpret a suggestion as criticism without much evidence. This moment is an opportunity for self-awareness and reflection. Why did you respond that way? What was the external factor? What was your emotional or reactive response? What could you have done differently? All of these are important questions to ask yourself not only in the moment but afterward as well. Critical thinking is used not only in conversations but also in outcomes.

Becoming aware of your own thinking patterns is like setting the GPS before starting a long journey. It's about knowing your starting point. Are you beginning your day with a mindset filled with assumptions, or are you open to new information and diverse perspectives? Recognizing these patterns isn't just an academic exercise; it has real-world implications. It affects how you interact with people, handle your job, and make all sorts of decisions—from choosing a meal to making financial investments.

Let's delve into some common thinking errors that can skew our judgment.

Overgeneralization

This is a frequent visitor in our thought processes. It happens when you take one or two instances and conclude that they represent a universal rule. Say you had a couple of bad experiences in group projects; you might find yourself thinking, "I always end up doing all the work in group settings." This is more than just an overstatement; it's an overgeneralization that might lead you to avoid teamwork, potentially missing out on valuable collaborative opportunities.

All-Or-Nothing Thinking

This is seeing things in black or white, with no middle ground. If you're not perfect, you're a failure—a harsh view that can set you up for significant stress and disappointment. Imagine you're launching a new product at work. If you expect it to be a market leader right out of the gate, you're setting yourself up for frustration. Life and business are rarely about absolutes; they're more often about finding viable paths forward in a landscape of grays.

Jumping to conclusions

This is yet another common cognitive shortcut that can lead us astray. It occurs when you make a decision without all the facts or interpret a situation based on insufficient evidence.

Suppose a friend doesn't return your call. In that case, you might conclude they're ignoring you when, in reality, they might simply be overwhelmed with other responsibilities.

The impact of such unchecked thinking patterns on your decisions and outcomes cannot be overstated. They can lead to poor decision-making, strained relationships, and missed opportunities. They can make you blind to potential risks or expose you to unnecessary risks, depending on the scenario. This is why identifying and understanding your own thinking patterns is not just an exercise; it's a necessary step toward enhancing your critical thinking skills. It's about building a foundation that allows you to engage more constructively and creatively with the challenges and decisions you face daily.

Recognizing these patterns in your thoughts is the first step toward change. It's about observing your mind and noticing when you're falling into these common traps. This awareness creates a space—a moment of choice—where you can decide to think differently. Instead of letting old patterns dictate your response, you can choose a more thoughtful, reasoned approach. This shift doesn't happen overnight. It requires practice and persistence. But the benefits of developing this kind of mental agility are profound. It not only enhances your ability to think critically but also empowers you to navigate your personal and professional worlds with greater confidence and effectiveness.

Keep these thoughts in mind as you continue to engage with this book. Reflect on your own experiences and notice when these patterns emerge. The more you practice, the more skilled you'll become at intercepting these automatic processes and transforming them into opportunities for deeper thinking and better decision-making. This isn't just about avoiding errors; it's about enhancing your ability to see more clearly, connect more deeply, and act more wisely.

1.4 THE ROLE OF LOGIC AND REASON IN CRITICAL THINKING

Imagine you're standing in a showroom, eyeing a sleek, new car. The salesperson approaches you with claims of unbeatable fuel efficiency and unmatched safety features. This is where logic and reason, the bedrock of critical thinking, come into play. Instead of taking the sales pitch at face value, you analyze the claims (logic) and assess their credibility (reason). This process is not just about debunking false claims or affirming factual ones; it's about engaging in a structured way of thinking that enables you to make informed decisions based on sound reasoning and valid arguments.

At its core, critical thinking is underpinned by logic and reason. These are not overly technical concepts reserved for philosophers and scientists but tools that we use daily, often without conscious thought. Logic, in its essence, is a systematic method of coming to a conclusion based on a set of premises. It is the framework within which reasoning takes place. Reasoning is the mental process of deriving logical conclusions from premises or evidence. Together, these elements form the foundation of critical thinking because they compel us to question, analyze, and evaluate—in other words, to think critically.

To grasp the role of logic in critical thinking, let's start with some basic logical structures that are used universally in reasoning. A common structure is the syllogism, which might sound intimidating but is something you've likely used without even realizing it. A syllogism is a form of reasoning where a conclusion is drawn from two given or assumed propositions (premises). A classic example is that all men are mortal (premise one). Socrates is a man (premise two). Therefore, Socrates is mortal (conclusion). This is an instance of deductive reasoning, where the conclusion logically follows from the premises, provided the premises are true.

Deductive reasoning (syllogism) is just one type of logical structure; inductive and abductive reasoning also play critical roles in forming logical bases in different scenarios.

Inductive reasoning involves making broad generalizations from specific observations—basically the reverse of deductive reasoning. For example, Every time I've eaten a strawberry, it's been sweet (premise one). I've eaten many strawberries in my life (premise two). Therefore, all strawberries are sweet (conclusion).

Abductive reasoning, often used in diagnostic processes like medical evaluations or fixing a car, involves starting with an incomplete set of observations and proceeding to the likeliest possible explanation. Understanding these structures is crucial because they are the tools that allow us to construct, deconstruct, and assess arguments critically and systematically.

Evaluating arguments is fundamental to critical thinking, particularly in an age where we are bombarded with information, opinions, and arguments from countless sources. To evaluate the strength of an argument, one must consider its logical soundness and validity. Logical soundness occurs when an argument is valid, and its premises are true, leading to a conclusion that is necessarily true. Validity, however, refers to the structure of the argument itself; it must be logically impeccable. For instance, if all premises of a valid argument are true, then the conclusion must be true. However, an argument can be valid even if its premises are false, which would lead to a false conclusion.

Referring to an earlier example, all humans are mortal (premise 1, **true**). Socrates is a human (premise 2, **true**). Therefore, Socrates is mortal (conclusion, **true**). This argument is valid because the conclusion logically follows from the premises, and all premises are true, leading to a true conclusion.

However, we can spin a different example to illustrate how arguing from a false premise can arrive at a false conclusion. For instance, All dogs can fly (premise 1, **false**). Socrates is a dog (premise 2, **false**). Therefore, Socrates can fly (conclusion, **false**). Even though both premises are false, the argument is still valid because the conclusion logically follows from the premises. However, since the premises are false, the conclusion is also false. This distinction is crucial in evaluating the various types of arguments we encounter daily.

While understanding valid and sound arguments is essential, recognizing logical fallacies is equally important. A logical fallacy is an error in reasoning that weakens arguments. They are deceptive and often persuasive, leading to faulty conclusions if not identified and countered. Common fallacies include:

- The straw man fallacy is where an opponent's argument is overstated or misrepresented to be easily attacked or refuted.
- The ad hominem fallacy is where the argument is directed against a person rather than the position they are maintaining.
- The appeal to ignorance asserts that a proposition is true because it has not yet been proven false, and vice versa.

These fallacies are pitfalls that can dramatically skew our understanding and hinder our ability to think critically if not recognized and addressed.

In your everyday life—whether you're evaluating a news article, a research paper, or a friend's opinion on a heated topic, your ability to apply logic and reason determines the quality of your conclusions. It's about making that mental shift from passively accepting information to actively questioning and analyzing its logic. This shift doesn't require you to be a philosopher or a scientist; it simply requires you to be an engaged, thoughtful individual committed to seeking truth and understanding in all aspects of life. As you continue to hone these skills, you'll find that your decisions become more informed, your judgments more sound, your conversations become more meaningful, and your understanding of the world more nuanced. This is the power of critical thinking, rooted in the timeless principles of logic and reason, adapted for the complex challenges of our modern world.

1.5 OVERCOMING THE FIRST HURDLE: ACKNOWLEDGING COGNITIVE BIASES

In the intricate tapestry of our thoughts and decisions, cognitive biases are like those stubborn knots that can distort the whole design if not carefully addressed. Cognitive bias influences our thinking and decision-making, leading us to process information selectively or subjectively, resulting in inaccurate or irrational judgment. They arise from various mental shortcuts—often called heuristics—that our brains use to process information quickly. While these shortcuts are beneficial in many situations, helping us make swift decisions in a complex world, they can also lead us astray, clouding our judgments with oversimplifications and inaccurate assumptions.

Understanding the nature of cognitive biases is crucial because it reveals a fundamental truth about human cognition: our thinking is not as objective as we might like to believe. Instead, it's shaped by a multitude of influences—emotional, social, and environmental—that can obscure our clarity without our conscious awareness.

Common Cognitive Biases:

Confirmation Bias. When making decisions, we often see what we expect to see, hear what we want to hear, and give more weight to information that confirms our preconceptions—a phenomenon known as confirmation bias. This bias can cause us to cherry-pick data or anecdotes that support our views, effectively putting on blinders to any contrary evidence.

Availability Heuristic. This is where we judge the likelihood of an event based on how easily examples come to mind. For instance, after hearing about a series of plane crashes, you might suddenly view air travel as more dangerous than it statistically is, simply because those dramatic events are more readily recalled than the countless safe flights that occur every day.

Anchoring Bias. This affects our ability to make judgments by over-relying on the first piece of information we encounter. If the first car you see at a dealership is priced at $30,000, any lower-priced car might seem like a bargain, even if its actual market value is much less.

These biases, while natural, can significantly impede our ability to think critically. They can skew our perceptions, lead us to make poor decisions and limit our understanding of the world and the people around us. However, the good news is that these biases can be managed with awareness and effort. One effective strategy to mitigate their influence is actively seeking out differing viewpoints. This doesn't just mean listening to or reading opinions that contrast with your own but genuinely trying to understand the reasoning behind these perspectives. It involves stepping outside your comfort zone and challenging your preconceptions, which can be as simple as conversing with someone from a different background or expertise. Ask yourself: why do they believe what they believe? What circumstances led them to that moment? Is there anything that they're saying I agree with, and why? Mentally walking a mile in another person's shoes is a simple yet effective way to shake yourself out of a cognitive bias you may have unknowingly developed.

Another practical approach is to question your initial assumptions. Before settling on a decision or forming an opinion, take a moment to scrutinize your reasoning. Ask yourself: What am I assuming here? Is there evidence to support these assumptions? Could I be wrong? This kind of questioning not only sharpens your critical thinking skills but also reduces the likelihood of biases steering your judgments.

However, it's important to recognize that overcoming cognitive biases isn't a one-time fix but a continuous effort. It requires persistent self-reflection and an openness to learning and growth. Every day presents new opportunities and challenges that can either entrench our biases or help us overcome them. By consciously recognizing and addressing our biases, we enhance our critical thinking abilities and contribute to more objective, balanced, and open-minded discussions in our personal and professional lives.

This ongoing process of recognizing and overcoming biases is akin to mental maintenance; just as a car needs regular checks to run smoothly, our thinking processes need continual attention and adjustment to function at their best. Each step we take to identify and counteract our biases is a step towards clearer thinking, better decision-making, and a deeper understanding of the complex world around us. As we move forward, remember that the goal is not to eliminate biases—as that is an impossible task given their deep-rooted nature in human cognition—but to manage them in a way that does not cloud our judgments or hinder our ability to think critically and make informed decisions.

Action Steps:

1. **Write down a logically sound/valid argument.**
2. **Write down a valid but not logically sound argument.**
3. **Write down a time when you observed yourself using "confirmation bias."**

CHAPTER 2
TOOLS FOR THOUGHT

Have you ever found yourself in a heated debate where, despite your best efforts, you end up arguing against a distorted version of your original statement? Or perhaps you've witnessed a political debate where candidates attack each other's character instead of discussing the policies? These are not just frustrating but classic examples of logical fallacies in action. Logical fallacies, the sneakiest of mental missteps, can turn a rational discussion into a pointless argument and can easily cloud judgment. This chapter will arm you with the tools needed to spot these fallacies in everyday life and avoid falling into their traps yourself.

2.1 INTRODUCTION TO LOGICAL FALLACIES

Definition and Importance

Logical fallacies are errors in reasoning that undermine the logic of an argument. They often sneak into debates and discussions, masquerading as solid points. Still, they reveal themselves to be false or deceptive upon closer inspection. Understanding logical fallacies is crucial because they can significantly impact the quality of your decisions and the persuasiveness of your arguments. They can distort your thinking, mislead your audience, and derail rational discussions. Identifying these logical fallacies is an important step in developing your strategic thinking abilities and a necessary one.

Types of Fallacies

Let's introduce some common types of logical fallacies you might encounter.

- *Ad Hominem* fallacy, where the argument is directed against a person rather than the position they are maintaining. For example, dismissing someone's argument by attacking their character or background instead of engaging with their points.
- *Straw Man* fallacy involves misrepresenting someone's argument to make it easier to attack. Imagine someone arguing that we should spend more on healthcare, and the response is, "He wants to use all the government money for healthcare and

leave nothing for education." That's a classic straw man—distorting the original point to make it seem unreasonable.

- *False Dilemma (Either/Or)* fallacy forces an unnecessary choice between two oversimplified options. "Either we ban all cars to save the environment, or we do nothing about pollution." This fallacy ignores the countless possible alternatives between the extremes.

Recognizing these types of fallacies in discussions can help you steer the conversation back to rational grounds or fortify your arguments against deceptive practices.

Identifying Fallacies

Identifying logical fallacies in everyday conversations requires attentiveness and a bit of skepticism. Start by listening carefully to how arguments are structured and what they are based upon. Are the conclusions drawn logically from the statements, or do they leap to generalizations? Does the speaker attack their opponent directly instead of addressing the argument? Are only two extreme options presented as the only possible solutions? Asking these questions can help you spot fallacies before they ruin or confuse the discussion.

To sharpen your skills, engage in mental simulations.

When you hear an argument:

- Try reconstructing it in your head.

- Break down the argument into its most basic premises.
- See if the conclusion logically follows.

This exercise can reveal hidden fallacies and strengthen your ability to think critically under pressure.

Avoiding Fallacies

Avoiding logical fallacies in your arguments requires a conscious effort to maintain clarity and integrity in your reasoning.

Here are a few things to look out for when examining your stance on something:

1. Always strive to attack the argument, not the person.
2. Make sure your conclusions are supported by evidence and follow logically from your premises.
3. Avoid oversimplifying complex issues into black-and-white choices.

Whenever you make a claim, ask yourself, "Am I backing this up with solid evidence, or am I just assuming it to be true?" This self-check can prevent fallacies from creeping into your own reasoning.

Another effective strategy is to invite feedback on your arguments. Sometimes, it's hard to spot our logical missteps, but a fresh pair of eyes can help pinpoint weaknesses in our reasoning. Engage friends or colleagues in friendly debates and encourage them to point out any fallacies. This helps refine your argumentative skills and enhances your critical thinking ability in collaborative settings.

Visual Element: Chart of Common Logical Fallacies

To help you better visualize and remember these fallacies, here is a simple chart categorizing some common logical fallacies, their definitions, and an example of each:

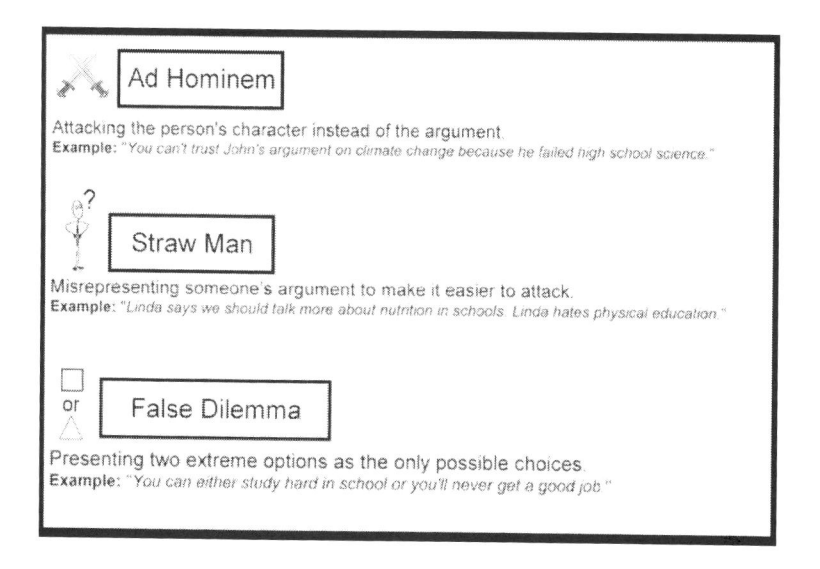

Ad Hominem
Attacking the person's character instead of the argument.
Example: "You can't trust John's argument on climate change because he failed high school science."

Straw Man
Misrepresenting someone's argument to make it easier to attack.
Example: "Linda says we should talk more about nutrition in schools. Linda hates physical education."

False Dilemma
Presenting two extreme options as the only possible choices.
Example: "You can either study hard in school or you'll never get a good job."

This chart serves as a quick reference that you can return to whenever you need to refresh your memory on these fallacies. By familiarizing yourself with these patterns, you can enhance your ability to engage in more productive and rational discussions, whether in personal conversations or professional debates.

2.2 THE ART OF ASKING THE RIGHT QUESTIONS

Have you heard the old adage, '*Knowledge is power*'? A better way to think about it might be, '*The ability to ask the right questions is power.*' In the realm of critical thinking, the questions we pose often determine the depth of understanding we reach. Questions are the engines of intellect, driving us past the surface of conventional thinking into the deeper waters of inquiry and insight. They encourage us to pause, ponder, and reflect, pushing us to challenge our assumptions and explore new perspectives.

Understanding the role of questioning in stimulating critical thinking is like learning how to mine for precious metals: You need the right tools and techniques to unearth the valuable ore buried beneath the surface. Questions serve as these tools, helping us dig deeper and uncover truths hidden within complex issues. When we ask a question, we're doing more than seeking information—inviting a deeper engagement with the topic at hand. We encourage ourselves and others to think more critically about the subject matter.

Differentiating between types of questions is crucial in this process. Open-ended and closed-ended questions serve different purposes and yield different types of information. Open-ended questions are broad and allow for various responses, inviting discussion and elaboration. They are the 'how' and 'why' questions that encourage deeper thinking and often lead to meaningful insights. For example, asking, "What strategies might we consider to improve our workflow?" opens up a discussion that can lead to creative and diverse solutions. On the other hand, closed-ended questions are more restrictive, typically requiring a simple, concise answer, often 'yes' or 'no.' These are useful for clarifying points and establishing facts quickly, such as asking, "Did everyone meet the project deadline?"

Strategic questioning is an art form that can significantly enhance the quality of dialogue and deliberation. It involves knowing what type of question to ask and when and how to ask it to elicit the most informative and honest responses. Effective questions often follow the principle of being clear, concise, and purposeful. They avoid ambiguity and are tailored to the context and the audience's knowledge level. For instance, strategically framing questions around specific objectives in a professional setting can help align a team's thinking and direct focus toward shared objectives. Teachers can use questions to draw out students' existing knowledge before introducing new concepts, connecting learning to students' experiences and reasoning.

Practical applications of strategic questioning are vast and varied. In personal interactions, asking thoughtful questions can help you build deeper relationships and better understand the perspectives of others. For example, instead of asking a partner, "Did you have a good day?" you might ask, "What was the most interesting part of your day?" This opens up a more engaging conversation and demonstrates a genuine interest in the details of their experiences. In professional contexts, strategic questioning can be used to nurture innovation and problem-solving. Questions can challenge the status quo and inspire a team to explore new possibilities. A leader might ask, "What if we approached this issue from a different angle? What are we missing?" Such questions can stimulate creative thinking and encourage a more thorough exploration of potential solutions.

In educational settings, the right questions can transform passive learning into an active exploration of knowledge. Teachers who master the art of questioning can engage students in deeper thinking and self-reflection, encouraging them to connect new knowledge with what they already know. For instance, in a history class, instead of asking students to simply list the causes of a historical event, a teacher might ask, "How might the outcome of this event have changed if this one factor had been different?" Such questions deepen students' understanding of the subject and improve their thinking ability.

In each of these examples, the power of questioning lies in seeking answers and fostering a deeper engagement with the world. Whether in personal conversations, professional projects, or educational environments, the questions we ask shape the paths of our inquiry and the scope of our understanding. They are fundamental tools in our critical thinking toolkit.

Personal Setting:

1. Instead of asking, "How was your day?" you could ask, "What made you smile today, even if just for a moment?" This question invites the person to share moments of joy or positivity, fostering a closer connection and brightening their mood.
2. Rather than asking, "What do you want to do this weekend?" try asking, "What's been tugging at

your heart lately? Something you've been itching to do or explore?" This question taps into the person's passions and desires, encouraging a more intimate conversation and potentially uncovering shared interests.
3. Instead of asking, "What's bothering you?" consider asking, "Is there a tiny step you can take today to ease any worries you have?" This gentle inquiry acknowledges the person's concerns while offering support and empowering them to take small, manageable actions toward resolution.

Professional Setting:

1. Instead of asking, "How can we improve productivity?" try asking, "What are the main bottlenecks hindering our workflow, and how can we address them strategically?" This question encourages a focused analysis of specific challenges and fosters a solutions-oriented approach among team members.
2. Rather than asking, "What's our next step?" consider asking, "What are the potential risks and opportunities associated with each course of action, and how can we prioritize them effectively?" This question promotes critical thinking and thorough evaluation of the implications of different decisions, guiding the team toward informed choices.
3. Instead of asking, "Who's responsible for this task?" try asking, "How can we leverage each team member's strengths to maximize efficiency and

collaboration on this project?" This question emphasizes teamwork and encourages a strategic allocation of resources based on individual capabilities, fostering a more cohesive and productive work environment.

Educational Setting:

1. Rather than asking, "What do you know about this topic?" try asking, "How do you think this concept applies to real-life situations you've encountered?" This question prompts students to relate academic knowledge to personal experiences, deepening their understanding and fostering critical thinking skills.
2. Instead of asking, "What's the answer?" consider asking, "What are the different approaches you could take to solve this problem, and what are the pros and cons of each?" This question encourages students to explore multiple strategies and consider the implications of their choices, promoting analytical thinking and problem-solving skills.
3. Rather than asking, "What did you learn from this lesson?" try asking, "How does this new knowledge challenge or reinforce your existing understanding of the subject?" This question encourages students to reflect on their learning process and make connections between new information and prior knowledge, fostering a deeper and more integrated understanding of the material.

2.3 STRATEGIES FOR EFFECTIVE ARGUMENT ANALYSIS

When you find yourself in a discussion, whether at a family dinner table, a team meeting, or during a community forum, the strength of your argument can either reinforce your position or cause your position to crumble. Understanding how to dissect an argument into its fundamental components is similar to a chef mastering the art of ingredient selection before creating a culinary masterpiece. Every argument is built from a series of premises that lead to a conclusion, often underpinned by various assumptions. Let's peel back these layers to see what makes an argument sound and compelling.

PREMISE

Firstly, every argument has premises, which are statements or facts assumed to be true and serve as the foundation for the conclusion. For example, if you argue that "We should invest more in renewable energy because it reduces pollution and is sustainable," your premises are that renewable energy reduces pollution and is sustainable. The conclusion you're driving at is that there should be more investment in renewable energy. Assumptions are the foundation of these premises. In this case, it might be assumed that reducing pollution is a desirable goal. Recognizing these elements helps clarify what's being argued and what needs to be proven or disproven.

EVIDENCE

Moving on to evaluating the evidence, this is where your critical thinking skills come into play. The quality and significance of the evidence supporting the premises of an argument can make or break its effectiveness. High-quality evidence is typically characterized by its source reliability, direct relevance to the argument, and currency. For instance, citing a recent, peer-reviewed scientific study that provides data on how renewable energy significantly cuts down pollution would strengthen your argument about renewable energy investment. On the other hand, outdated statistics or sources from questionable origins would weaken it. Always ask yourself: Is this evidence reliable? Is it directly related to the premise? Is it the most current information available?

STRENGTH

Assessing the strength of an argument is next. This does not solely rest on the logical structure, coherence, and supporting evidence. A strong argument is logically valid—meaning the conclusion necessarily follows from the premises—and sound, where all premises are true. Furthermore, the argument should be coherent, connecting all points and sub-arguments without contradictions. For instance, if another part of your argument against non-renewable energy sources contradicts your data or logic about renewable resources, this incoherence weakens your overall position. Always review your argument for logical fallacies, inconsistencies, or exaggerated claims that could undermine your main point.

CONSTRUCT

Lastly, constructing strong arguments is a skill that improves with practice and intention. Start with clearly defined premises:

- Make sure they are not only true but are also accepted as true by your audience or can be easily supported by strong evidence.
- Structure your argument in a way that logically leads to your conclusion.
- Avoid making leaps in logic or leaving gaps that require the listener to make unjustified connections.
- Clarity and conciseness are your allies when presenting your argument, whether in writing or speech. Keep your language simple, and your points well-ordered. This helps maintain your audience's focus and prevents misunderstandings.
- Anticipate counterarguments. By proactively addressing potential criticisms of your argument, you strengthen your position and show a well-rounded understanding of the topic.

In all these steps, the effectiveness of your argument hinges not just on the solid ground of logic and evidence but also on your ability to communicate clearly and respond to feedback dynamically. Whether you're persuading, debating, or simply informing, these strategies lay the groundwork for making your arguments heard, respected, and considered.

2.4 LEVERAGING HEURISTICS FOR BETTER DECISION-MAKING

Imagine you're walking down a busy street looking for a place to eat. You notice a restaurant buzzing with customers while another is nearly empty. Without knowing anything else, you might choose the busier one, assuming its popularity equates to better quality. This mental shortcut is known as a heuristic. Heuristics are cognitive strategies or 'rules of thumb' that simplify decision-making by reducing the complex task of assessing probabilities and predicting values to more manageable judgments. These mental shortcuts are used to speed up the decision-making process and are particularly useful in complex environments where time is of the essence and immediate decisions are necessary.

Heuristics play a pivotal role in everyday decision-making. They help us navigate the endless stream of choices without overwhelming our cognitive resources.

- **Availability Heuristic** relies on immediate examples that come to a given person's mind when evaluating a specific topic, concept, method, or decision. The ease with which something can be recalled from memory is used to indicate how often or how likely it is. Suppose you frequently hear about airplane accidents on the news. In that case, you might overestimate the danger of flying despite statistics that say it's one of the safest modes of transportation.
- **Representativeness Heuristic**, where people judge the probability or frequency of an event by the extent that the event resembles the typical case. For example, suppose someone is described as young, energetic, and loves listening to loud music. In that case, you might quickly conclude they're a student based on how well they fit your stereotype

of what a student is typically like rather than considering other possibilities.

While heuristics can significantly ease the burden of decision-making, they are not without their pitfalls. Over-reliance on these mental shortcuts can lead to systematic deviations from logic, probability, or rational choice theory. The main risk is that while heuristics are generally helpful, they can sometimes lead to severe errors or biases.

For example:

- **Confirmation Bias** is the tendency to look for, interpret, and remember information in a way that aligns with one's existing beliefs or assumptions while giving significantly less attention to other possibilities. This bias can prevent individuals from noticing information that might be more critical or more accurate, leading to poor decision-making.

Balancing heuristics with analytical thinking is crucial for making sound decisions. While heuristics provide a quick, often effective route to everyday decision-making, they are most effective when used in conjunction with thorough analysis, especially when the stakes are high. To strike this balance, it's essential first to recognize when you're using a heuristic and then determine whether it's the best tool for the decision at hand. For instance, if you're making a significant investment, relying solely on the familiarity heuristic (choosing the most familiar options) might not be wise. In such cases, it might be beneficial to complement your heuristic judgment with detailed analysis, such as researching market trends, seeking expert advice, and considering long-term impacts.

One effective strategy for balancing intuitive heuristics with detailed analysis is to set predefined rules or criteria for when to use each approach. Heuristics can be incredibly efficient for decisions that have low impact and require quick action. However, a more analytical approach might be necessary for more complex, high-stakes decisions. Furthermore, fostering an environment that encourages questioning and critical evaluation can help mitigate the risks associated with over-reliance on heuristics. Encouraging yourself and others to ask questions like "What am I missing here?" or "Is there a reason I feel this way that isn't immediately obvious?" can help uncover hidden biases and lead to better decision outcomes.

In practice, combining heuristics with analysis might look like using your instinct to make a preliminary choice but then validating this choice with data and logical reasoning. For example, suppose you decide between two job offers. In that case, you might instinctively prefer one over the other because it feels like a better cultural fit (affect heuristic). However, before making a final decision, you would compare the benefits, responsibilities, career growth opportunities, and other tangible factors. This approach ensures that your decision is fast, efficient but also robust, and well-rounded, thereby harnessing the best of both intuitive and analytical worlds in your decision-making process.

2.5 MIND MAPPING FOR COMPLEX PROBLEM SOLVING

The traditional list-making approach might fall short when faced with a complex problem or a complicated project. This is where mind mapping comes into play—an innovative and highly visual method that helps you organize your thoughts and ideas more effectively. Mind mapping isn't just about jotting down what you need to do; it's about visually structuring your thoughts to reflect the connections of various elements and ideas. This method is particularly beneficial because it mirrors the way our brains naturally operate by associating ideas with each other directly, side by side, rather than keeping them in a bullet point list.

Mind mapping starts with a central concept or idea in the middle of a blank page. From this center, branches are drawn outwards in all directions, representing major themes or tasks related to the central concept. Each branch can then be extended to include smaller, related tasks or ideas, creating a sprawling visual representation of complex information. This technique helps organize and retain information more effectively and stimulates creative thinking and problem-solving. By visually laying out all aspects of a problem, you can see the relationships between the different parts, identify areas that need more exploration, and pinpoint redundancies or contradictions.

The process of creating a mind map is quite straightforward and remarkably impactful. Start by identifying the central theme or problem and place it at the center of your page. From there, draw branches that represent the main categories or subtopics related to your central theme. Use single words or short phrases for these branches to keep the map clean and readable. Extend these branches into finer details, adding sub-branches for more specific tasks or ideas. As you branch out, use different colors or symbols to categorize or prioritize information, which adds an additional layer of organization and helps in quick visual scanning. You can also add images or sketches to your mind map, which can be especially useful for visual learners or to express more spatial or abstract ideas.

Image Example:

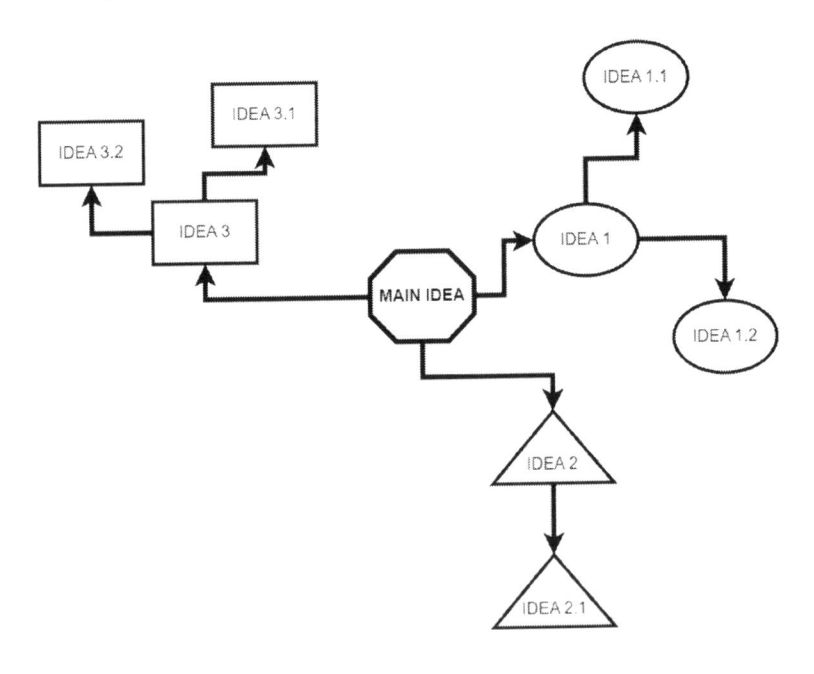

Mind mapping can be applied effectively across various settings, enhancing both personal and professional efficiency. In a personal context, for instance, you might use a mind map to plan a major event like a family reunion, outlining everything from the guest list to the menu to activities, each with its own sub-branch detailing all necessary actions and considerations. In educational settings, mind maps can be a powerful tool for students to plan out essays or projects, helping them organize their research and structure their thoughts. Teachers can even use mind maps as a teaching aid to visually represent complex subjects, helping students to see the 'bigger picture' and understand how different facts and ideas are connected.

In the professional realm, mind mapping proves invaluable in project management and strategic planning. It allows teams to brainstorm ideas and visualize the scope of a project, including tasks, deadlines, and dependencies. This can lead to more effective meetings and collaboration, as everyone can see the plan and understand how their work fits into the overall project. Additionally, mind maps can be used in presentations to communicate complex information in a clear, engaging, and visually appealing manner, making it easier for the audience to follow and retain the information presented.

Mind mapping helps organize thoughts and ideas efficiently and significantly enhances critical thinking. Visually organizing your information can enhance your strategic thinking and make it easier to identify gaps or biases in your thought process or argument. This visual arrangement encourages you to think outside the box and see new pathways and connections that might not be as obvious in a more linear format like text. The interactive nature of mind mapping—where you can easily add, adjust, or remove ideas—also makes it a dynamic tool for critical thinking, allowing you to refine your thoughts continuously as you gain more information or clarity.

As you continue to explore and apply mind mapping to various aspects of your life, you'll likely discover more personal and unique ways to adapt this tool to suit your specific needs and challenges. Whether it's planning a personal project, facilitating a brainstorming session, or structuring a complex argument, mind mapping offers a versatile and effective strategy to enhance your thinking and problem-solving capabilities.

As we wrap up this exploration of mind mapping, remember that this tool is just one of many in your critical thinking arsenal. Each method or technique offers unique benefits and can be particularly effective in certain situations. The key is to remain flexible and open to various approaches, using them to enhance your understanding, solve problems, and make decisions more effectively.

Action Steps:

- **Write down the last time you used a fallacy in a discussion (Ad Hominem/Straw Man/False Dilemma).**
- **Write down a question you used to ask but now ask in a different way using the guidance of this chapter.**
- **Create your own example of a mind map.**

CHAPTER 3
RATIONAL THINKING IN THE DIGITAL AGE

Navigating the vast digital landscape can sometimes feel like trying to find your way through a bustling city market—every stall and vendor competes for your attention, each claiming to offer the best or the most authentic experience. In such a setting, critical thinking becomes your most reliable tool for discerning which vendors are genuine and which ones are not. Similarly, in the digital age, where information is plentiful and not always policed, critical thinking becomes your most reliable tool. This chapter is dedicated to sharpening that tool, especially in the context of evaluating online sources. Let's dive into how you can become a more discerning consumer of digital content, enhancing your ability to separate fact from fiction.

3.1 EVALUATING ONLINE SOURCES: A PRACTICAL APPROACH

Criteria for Credibility

When you come across a piece of information online, it's like coming across a storefront's appealing display. Before you decide to invest time or money into what you see, you need to assess its credibility. Start by examining the source. Is it reputable? Look for indications of the source's authority on the subject, such as affiliations with respected institutions or a history of reliable reporting. Check the publication date; is the information current, or could it be outdated and possibly irrelevant? Also, scrutinize the evidence supporting the claims. Reliable sources typically back up their claims with verifiable evidence, providing links to research or citing known experts. Another aspect to consider is the purpose of the information. Ask yourself: Is this content intended to inform, entertain, persuade, or sell? Understanding the purpose can provide insights into potential biases and help you gauge the impartiality of the information presented.

Fact-checking Techniques

Once you've assessed the credibility of the source, the next step is to verify the facts. This is where effective fact-checking techniques come into play. Start by cross-referencing the information with other credible sources. If the claim is factual, other reputable publications or official sources should corroborate it. Utilize established fact-checking websites; these platforms specialize in debunking false claims and providing contextual truths. Additionally, many modern-day search engines allow you to do a reverse image search, using an image you have on your computer or phone and finding images like it. This can be an important tool when determining the authenticity of an image, especially with the rise of AI and digital image manipulation. Remember, effective fact-checking often requires looking beyond the first page of search engine results and delving deeper into academic journals, books, and official reports that may not be as readily accessible but offer an abundance of reliable information.

Recognizing Bias

Recognizing bias in digital content is similar to detecting a sleight of hand in a magic show—it's about paying attention to what might be subtly influencing perceptions.

Bias can appear in many forms, such as:

- Word choice
- Omission of certain facts
- Framing information in a way that leans towards a particular viewpoint.

To spot these biases, consider the language used—is it emotive, suggestive, or loaded with value judgments? Analyze the balance of the content; does it present multiple viewpoints, or does it seem to push a single perspective? Seeking diverse sources is also vital in offsetting bias; expose yourself to different viewpoints and media outlets, especially those that challenge your preconceptions. This not only broadens your understanding but also sharpens your ability to critically evaluate arguments and claims.

Biased Statement:

"The new smartphone's pathetic battery life makes it a terrible choice for anyone who needs a reliable device."

Analysis of Bias:

Emotive Language: Words like "pathetic" and "terrible" are emotionally charged and convey strong negative judgments.

Lack of Balance: The statement focuses only on the negative aspect (battery life) without mentioning any positive features or comparing it to alternatives.

Framing: The information is framed to create a negative impression of the smartphone, rather than providing a balanced review.

By mastering these skills—evaluating credibility, fact-checking, and recognizing bias—you equip yourself with the necessary tools to navigate the digital world more confidently and skillfully. Whether you're researching for work, verifying news stories, or just satisfying personal curiosity, these skills ensure that you can stand firm on the solid ground of truth, even as the tides of digital content shift around you.

3.2 SOCIAL MEDIA AND CRITICAL THINKING: BEYOND THE ECHO CHAMBER

Social media platforms have transformed into the modern-day public squares where ideas, news, and personal beliefs converge and contend. However, these platforms can also act as echo chambers—environments where you mostly encounter views that reinforce your existing beliefs. Companies curate your newsfeed, advertisements, and display content based on your search history, links you've clicked, and items you've shopped online for. This is your algorithm--your digital footprint--and can be used to reinforce the walls of your echo chamber--consistently feeding you content that companies think you will like. Unfortunately, this can lead to an increase in bias (even a subconscious one) and requires regular effort to find stories and news that are **not** curated for you.

To navigate social media more critically and escape the attraction of echo chambers, it's crucial to engage with content critically. This involves actively questioning the assumptions that underlie what you read and watch. For instance, when you come across a viral post or a trending video, take a moment to ask:

- What is the message here?
- Who benefits from this message?
- What might be left unsaid?
- Why is it left unsaid?

This practice helps you to peel back layers of content that might initially seem straightforward but are often laced with subtleties and nuances aimed at swaying your opinion. Additionally, cross-referencing the information you find on social media with reputable sources can provide a broader perspective and help verify the accuracy of what you're consuming. This can apply to news articles, blogs, videos, and even user comments. Many of these mediums, and more, can carry misleading or one-sided information intending to push a specific narrative.

Building a diverse social media feed is another effective strategy for breaking out of echo chambers. Start by following a range of content creators, activists, thought leaders, and news outlets with varying perspectives. If the digital space you occupy is only pushing one idealogy, or one political message, you may want to seek out voices and views from the opposite spectrum to form a well-rounded view of events. Follow international sources to get a global view of issues, and subscribe to channels that focus on data-driven analysis, which can provide a more objective take on contentious topics. Additionally, platforms often allow you to customize your news feed preferences; use these tools to ensure you're not just seeing the most popular posts but a wide range of content that challenges and broadens your worldview.

Mindful consumption of social media is perhaps the most crucial aspect of engaging with digital content. It involves recognizing not only how and what you consume online, but also when to step away. Continuous exposure to information, especially if it's emotionally charged or controversial, can lead to fatigue and affect your ability to think critically. It's important to recognize signs of feeling overwhelmed. Recognizing thoughts of anxiety, or agitation, is important when navigating any space, and crucial for curating critical thinking. Sometimes, that could even be what the content is trying to do: irritate or excite you, so you think less critically about the position they're trying to sell. These are signals that it might be time to take a break. Use features like "screen time" tools to monitor how much time you spend on social platforms and set limits if necessary.

By actively striving to understand and navigate the complexities of social media through these strategies, you become better equipped to use these powerful platforms not just as a consumer of information, but as a discerning participant in the global dialogue. This shift is not just about enhancing your individual critical thinking skills; it's about contributing to a more informed, open, and thoughtful digital community.

3.3 THE DANGERS OF MISINFORMATION AND HOW TO COMBAT THEM

Misinformation can be compared to weeds in a garden; if left unchecked, it can spread quickly and choke out valuable plants. In this case, the valuable plants being truthful information. In its essence, misinformation refers to false or inaccurate information that is spread, regardless of the intent to deceive. Its impact on society is far-reaching, influencing everything from everyday decisions to national policies.

Misinformation can create:

1. Confusion.
2. Distrust.
3. Polarize opinions.
4. And in severe cases, incite violence.

Its ability to distort public perception and influence social and political climates makes understanding and combating misinformation a critical skill, especially in today's digital age.

One might wonder why misinformation is so widespread and compelling. Its sources are as varied as they are numerous, ranging from social media platforms and online forums to some news outlets and influential public figures. Part of its persuasion lies in its design; it often taps into existing fears, biases, or desires, making the false information seem more believable or appealing. For example, during election cycles, misinformation might play into fears about economic instability or job security, swaying public opinion with sensational but unfounded claims. Additionally, the algorithms governing much of our digital consumption tend to favor content that generates strong emotional responses, regardless of its veracity. This means that misinformation, which is often sensational, can spread much faster and further than mundane, factual content.

Combating misinformation requires a proactive and diverse approach. First and foremost, critical questioning is an indispensable tool. Whenever you encounter new information, especially if it elicits a strong emotional response or seems too good (or bad) to be true, take a moment to question its source, intent, and evidence.

Ask yourself:

- Who benefits from this information?
- What sources are cited, and are they trustworthy?

- Is this information being used to sell something, literal or figurative?

These questions can help you peel back the layers of possible deceptions or mistakes. Moreover, strengthening your fact-checking skills is crucial. This doesn't just mean checking if other sources agree but assessing the reliability of those sources themselves. Often, it can be helpful to research whether a news outlet or blog is owned by a parent company of a product or article they are covering. For example: The local newspaper, The Paper, is running a hard-hitting article on the dangerous microfibers found in a new type of carpet from the company, Fabulous Carpet. However, when you dig deeper, you find that The Paper is owned by the same company that *also* owns a carpet competitor to Fabulous Carpet. This doesn't mean there couldn't be dangerous microfibers in the new carpet, but you need to verify the information from multiple unaffiliated sources. Reputable fact-checking services can be invaluable here, as they provide unbiased evaluations of claims and can help clarify what's true, false, or somewhere in between.

Personal responsibility plays a pivotal role in curbing the spread of misinformation. In an age where sharing information is as easy as clicking a button, each of us has a duty to ensure that what we share is accurate and harmless. This responsibility extends beyond not sharing false information; it involves actively correcting misinformation when you encounter it, especially if it's shared by someone you know. Educating others about the importance of verifying information before sharing it can also help cultivate a more informed and discerning online community. Additionally, supporting institutions and platforms that prioritize accuracy over sensationalism can drive a collective shift towards more reliable and trustworthy information distribution.

In your daily interactions with digital content, remember that your actions have power. By choosing to verify before sharing, to question before accepting, and to educate rather than ignore, you contribute to a culture of truth and responsibility. These actions might seem small in the moment, but collectively, they can significantly reduce the spread of dangerous misinformation, leading to a more informed and rational public discourse. As you navigate the complexities of the digital age, let your critical thinking skills light the way, helping you discern truth in a sea of misinformation and empowering you to make decisions based on accurate and reliable information.

3.4 DIGITAL LITERACY: THINKING CRITICALLY ABOUT TECHNOLOGY'S ROLE IN OUR LIVES

In today's fast-evolving tech landscape, being digitally literate is as crucial as learning to read or write. Digital literacy isn't just about knowing how to use technology; it's about understanding how to navigate its complexities safely and effectively. This involves a mix of skills including, but not limited to:

- Understanding how digital content is created.
- Comprehending the underlying technologies that power what we use.

- Being aware of the ethical and security implications of our digital actions.

To be digitally literate means you're equipped to handle the digital aspects of your daily life—from knowing how to manage your online identity to understanding the implications of sharing information on social media platforms. It also means recognizing how digital media can influence and manipulate personal and public opinion and how to interact online in a way that respects your own privacy and that of others. For instance, when you download a new app, digital literacy helps you understand what permissions the app asks for, like access to your camera, microphone, or location, and what implications these permissions have for your privacy.

Balancing the benefits and drawbacks of technology is a critical skill in digital literacy. On one hand, technology can vastly improve our lives—think of the ease of online banking, the breadth of knowledge available at our fingertips, and the ability to connect with people across the globe in an instant. On the other hand, these conveniences come with risks—cybersecurity threats, misinformation, and potential impacts on mental health, to name a few. To use technology critically and responsibly, you need to be able to weigh these benefits and risks. For example, consider the convenience of wearable technology that tracks personal health data against the potential for sensitive information to be accessed by unauthorized parties. A digitally literate person can navigate these waters by setting up proper security measures, like two-factor authentication and secure passwords, and by being judicious about what information to share and where.

Privacy and security are pillars of digital literacy. Understanding how your data is collected, used, and shared online is crucial. This isn't just about knowing what information you are giving access to but also understanding how that information could be used—for good or evil. Every piece of data shared can paint a detailed picture of a person's life, which can be used to tailor marketing strategies, influence political campaigns, or even perpetrate identity theft. Therefore, part of being digitally literate involves staying informed about the latest security practices and understanding the privacy policies of the platforms you use. It's about making informed choices concerning the digital products and services you engage with daily.

Looking to the future, the role of technology and, consequently, the importance of digital literacy will only grow. Emerging technologies like artificial intelligence, blockchain, and quantum computing will create new opportunities and challenges. These technologies will transform how we live, work, and interact, making it even more critical to remain not just informed, but critically engaged with technological developments. Future trends suggest a world where digital literacy will be indispensable. The ability to adapt to new technologies, to understand their implications, and to navigate their potential impacts on society will be crucial. Critical thinking, as always, will be at the heart of this adaptation—ensuring that as technology advances, it does so in a way that benefits society as a whole without infringing on individual rights and freedoms.

In summary, the journey through digital literacy is ongoing and ever-evolving. It's about more than just using technology

—it's about understanding its role in our lives and its potential to affect change. As we continue to integrate technology more deeply into every aspect of our daily activities, the need for robust digital literacy becomes more apparent. This chapter has set the foundation, equipping you with the knowledge to navigate the digital age responsibly and effectively. As you continue to the next chapter, carry forward the understanding that your actions online shape not just your own digital footprint but the digital landscape itself, influencing how technology will evolve and impact generations to come.

Disengaging from someone online who lacks civility or intends to troll is essential to maintaining a healthy digital environment. Much like avoiding a poisonous plant that can harm your well-being, it's important to recognize when an online interaction is unproductive or harmful. When faced with hostility or trolling, prioritize your mental and emotional health by not engaging with inflammatory comments. Instead, focus on setting boundaries; politely state your intent not to engage in disrespectful discourse and then refrain from responding further. Utilize platform tools such as blocking or reporting to minimize your exposure to toxic interactions. Remember, engaging with trolls only fuels their behavior, but by choosing not to participate, you contribute to a more respectful and constructive online space.

Exercise: Practicing Credibility Assessment

To put these concepts into practice, try the following exercise: Choose a current topic that interests you and find three different articles from three different sources on this topic. Apply the criteria for credibility to each source: check the authority of the authors, the timeliness of the articles, the evidence supporting the claims, and the purpose of the articles. Then, use fact-checking techniques to verify key facts mentioned in the articles. Finally, write down any biases you might have noticed in each article. Reflect on how these biases could influence a reader's understanding of the topic. This exercise will help you hone your ability to critically assess online content, making you a more informed and rational consumer of digital information.

Action Steps:

- **Assess Source Credibility:** The next time you read an article or social media post, take a moment to investigate the source.
- **Cross-Reference Information:** When you come across a surprising or sensational claim, don't take it at face value. Search for the same information on multiple reputable websites or news outlets.
- **Reflect on Emotional Reactions:** If a piece of digital content elicits a strong emotional response, pause and reflect on why that might be. Ask yourself who benefits from this message and what might be left unsaid. Write down your response, and revisit it in a few days or weeks. Does it still seem true to you?

CHAPTER 4
PROBLEM SOLVING IN PERSONAL DECISIONS

Imagine standing at a crossroads, each path leading to vastly different landscapes of life. Whether it's choosing a career, buying a home, or pursuing further education, these aren't just mere choices; they are pivotal decisions that shape the trajectory of your life. Every decision presents a unique opportunity, not just to select a path but to harness the power of critical thinking to sculpt your future. This chapter is your guide to transforming these decision-making moments from daunting forks in the road to empowering milestones in your personal growth journey.

4.1 NAVIGATING LIFE'S BIG DECISIONS WITH CRITICAL THOUGHT

Decisions as Opportunities

Every significant decision carries weight—the weight of uncertainty, potential, and change. However, viewing decisions through a lens of opportunity can dramatically shift your approach. Instead of a source of stress, each decision becomes a chance to apply your critical thinking skills, enabling you to navigate through complexities with more confidence and clarity. This perspective turns the decision-making process into a proactive exercise in personal development, where each choice contributes to your growth as a discerning, thoughtful individual.

Frameworks for Decision-Making

To systematically approach the complexities of big decisions, several decision-making frameworks can guide your critical thinking. One such tool is the SWOT analysis, which stands for

- **S**trengths
- **W**eaknesses
- **O**pportunities
- **T**hreats

This framework helps you map out the internal and external factors that could impact your decision. For instance, when considering a career change, a SWOT analysis allows you to evaluate your professional skills (strengths and weaknesses) alongside market demand and industry trends (opportunities and threats).

Another technique is cost-benefit analysis, which involves weighing the anticipated costs against the benefits of a potential decision. This method isn't just about numbers; it's about value. For example, when deciding whether to buy a home, the cost isn't merely the price of the property but also includes factors like maintenance expenses and mortgage interest. The benefits would include home equity, privacy, and personal satisfaction. By clearly laying out the costs and benefits, you can make a decision that aligns with both your financial and personal goals.

Case Studies

To illustrate the application of critical thinking in real-life decisions, consider the following scenarios:

- **Career Choice**: Emily is contemplating a shift from a corporate job to starting her own business. Using SWOT, she identifies her strong entrepreneurial skills and unique business ideas as strengths. Her lack of experience in business management poses a weakness. The growing market for her product represents an opportunity, while a big box store that sells a competing product which plans to open near her stands as a threat. Through this analysis, Emily decides to take business management courses to mitigate her weaknesses, and to work with a marketing company

to properly establish her product as different from the competition to lessen the threat.
- **Buying a Home**: John and Rita are deciding whether to buy a house. They perform a cost-benefit analysis by comparing the long-term benefits of home ownership, such as asset appreciation and tax advantages, against the costs, including initial down payment, ongoing maintenance, and property taxes. This thorough analysis reassures them that buying a house aligns with their long-term financial and family planning goals.

Long-term Thinking

The importance of considering long-term impacts cannot be overstressed in decision-making. Often, the full consequences of our decisions unfold only with time. By incorporating long-term thinking into your decision-making process, you ensure that your choices address immediate needs and set you up for future success. This involves looking beyond the immediate effects and considering how your decision will influence your life in five, ten, or even twenty years. It's about aligning your decisions with your broader life goals and values, ensuring that each choice you make is a step towards the future you want.

In the upcoming sections, we will explore other critical areas of personal decision-making, such as financial planning, health and wellness, relationship management, and parental guidance in fostering critical thinking among children. Each of these areas requires a tailored approach to problem-solving and decision-making, which will be discussed in detail.

4.2 BUDGETING AND FINANCIAL PLANNING THROUGH LOGICAL ANALYSIS

Financial Literacy Basics

Let's set the foundation with some financial literacy basics, which are essential tools for anyone looking to take control of their finances. While this book is not about providing in-depth financial knowledge or advice, understanding the fundamentals of financial literacy involves getting to grips with concepts such as budgeting, saving, investing, and understanding credit. These concepts are not just about numbers; they reflect your financial health and influence your ability to make informed financial decisions. For instance, knowing how interest rates work can save you from the pitfalls of bad debt, while understanding investment principles can help you build wealth over time. Financial literacy empowers you to be able to more effectively navigate and understand the results of the decisions you make.

Analyzing Financial Habits

Now, think about your daily financial habits. How often do you track your spending? Do you know where your money goes each month? Analyzing your financial habits is the first step towards gaining control over your finances. Start by tracking your expenses for a month. Categorize your spending into essentials and non-essentials. Essentials include rent, utilities, groceries, and transportation costs, while non-essentials might include dining out, entertainment, and luxury purchases. This exercise isn't about judging your spending but about observing patterns. You might discover, for instance, that a significant portion of your budget goes to subscriptions you rarely use or impulsive online purchases. By critically analyzing these habits, you can identify areas where adjustments can lead to improved financial health.

Creating a Budget

Creating a budget that aligns with your personal goals and values is like drawing a map that guides you to your financial destination. Start by listing all your income sources, followed by your expenses, categorized as mentioned earlier. Ensure your essentials are covered first, then allocate a portion of what remains to savings. Feel free to adjust the amounts allocated to better fit your financial objectives and lifestyle. For instance, if you're saving for a down payment on a house or aiming to pay off debt quickly, you might want to funnel more into savings and cut back on non-essentials. A budget is not set in stone; it's a flexible tool that should adapt to changes in your financial situation and priorities.

Strategic Financial Planning

Strategic financial planning is about setting long-term financial goals and outlining steps to achieve them. This process involves more than just saving money each month; it requires a clear vision of what you want to achieve and a structured plan to get there. Begin by defining clear, actionable financial goals. These could range from paying off student loans within five years to saving for retirement or setting up an emergency fund. Prioritize these goals based on urgency and importance, and then break them down into smaller, manageable steps. For example, if your goal is to build an emergency fund, decide on the total amount you need to save and establish a monthly saving goal that fits into your budget.

Additionally, consider potential financial risks and think about ways to mitigate them. This might involve diversifying your investment portfolio or getting appropriate insurance coverage. Strategic financial planning isn't just about growing your wealth; it's about making thoughtful decisions that secure your financial future and give you the freedom to enjoy the fruits of your labor without undue stress.

By integrating these elements—solid financial literacy, a habit of analyzing spending, a well-structured budget, and strategic financial planning—you equip yourself with a robust toolkit for managing your personal finances. This approach not only enhances your current financial well-being but also paves the way for sustained financial health and freedom. As you continue to apply these principles, you'll find that financial decision-making becomes less intimidating and more empowering, allowing you to tackle other areas of personal decision-making with increased confidence and clarity.

4.3 HEALTH AND WELLNESS DECISIONS SIMPLIFIED

With the immense amount of health information available today, from online articles to fitness gurus on social media, distinguishing solid advice from sensational claims can feel overwhelming. This section will help provide you with practical strategies to critically evaluate health information, enabling you to make informed and effective decisions about your health and wellness. Whether you're considering a new diet trend, an exercise routine, or a medical treatment, the ability to sift through and assess the reliability and relevance of the information you encounter is crucial.

When evaluating health information, especially online, start by considering the source. Trusted health websites typically have affiliations with accredited health institutions or are directly linked to recognized medical professionals. Check the author's credentials and whether the content is reviewed by medical professionals before publication. Another critical aspect is the evidence supporting the claims. Reliable health information should reference scientific studies, clinical trials, or statistical data that can be verified through respected medical journals or databases like *PubMed*, which is a repository of research and clinical papers, and should be a reliable source for most research inquiries. Be wary of articles that rely heavily on personal stories or testimonials without citing scientific evidence. Also, watch out for red flags like sensational headlines or promises of quick fixes, which often indicate that the content is more about clickbait than actual health advice.

Making informed health choices extends beyond just identifying credible sources. It involves a deeper understanding of your own health needs and goals. For instance, when choosing a diet, consider not just the popularity of the diet but how well it aligns with your nutritional needs, lifestyle, and any existing medical conditions. Consult with healthcare professionals before adopting any new diet, especially if it involves significant changes in your current eating habits. The same goes for exercise programs; what works for a fitness influencer might not be appropriate for your fitness level or health conditions. Remember, the best health choices are those that consider your unique circumstances and are based on a blend of credible information and professional advice.

Debunking health myths and misconceptions is another area where critical thinking is invaluable. Many health myths persist because they are often rooted in half-truths. For instance, the myth that eating carbs always leads to weight gain ignores the complexities of how carbohydrates affect the body and the role they play in a balanced diet. To debunk such myths, it's essential to research and understand the scientific principles involved. Look for information from sources that not only state the facts but also explain the reasoning and science behind them. This understanding will allow you to make decisions based on science rather than popular but potentially misleading conceptions.

Lastly, adopting a preventative health mindset is perhaps the most strategic application of critical thinking to health and wellness. This approach focuses on making lifestyle choices that prevent illness before it starts rather than treating symptoms after they arise. Preventative health involves regular health screenings, a balanced diet, regular physical activity, and mental health management. By thinking critically about preventative health, you assess the long-term benefits of lifestyle choices and how they contribute to your overall well-being. It's about making conscious decisions that address immediate health concerns and proactively safeguard your future health.

Navigating health and wellness decisions with a critical eye doesn't just lead to better health outcomes; it also fosters a more empowered and proactive approach to managing your health. By learning to evaluate information critically, make informed decisions, debunk myths, and prioritize preventative care, you equip yourself with the tools to lead a healthier, more balanced life.

4.4 CRITICAL THINKING IN RELATIONSHIPS: DECODING CONVERSATIONS AND BEHAVIORS

Navigating the complex maze of human relationships requires more than just good intentions; it demands a keen understanding of different communication styles and an ability to interpret messages accurately. In your daily interactions, whether with a partner, a colleague, or a friend, you'll encounter a diverse array of communication styles. Some people express themselves directly, leaving little to interpretation, while others might communicate in more subtle, indirect ways. Recognizing these styles is the first step in ensuring effective communication. For instance, a direct communicator values straightforwardness and might become frustrated with vague responses, whereas an indirect communicator might feel overwhelmed or pressured by too direct an approach. By applying critical thinking, you can adapt your communication strategy to suit the style of the person you're interacting with, which not only fosters better understanding but also enhances the quality of your interactions.

When conflicts arise, as they inevitably do in relationships, critical thinking becomes an indispensable tool in resolving them constructively. The key here is active listening, which involves fully concentrating on what is being said rather than just passively hearing the message. This technique allows you to deeply understand the other person's perspective, which is crucial in conflict resolution. When you actively listen, you're not preparing your rebuttal or planning your next argument; instead, you're focused on understanding the underlying issues that have led to the conflict. This approach can be complemented by questioning assumptions, both yours and the other person's. Often, conflicts are based on misunderstood intentions or unfounded beliefs about each other's motives. By questioning these assumptions, you can uncover the real issues at hand and address them directly, which leads to more effective and lasting resolutions.

Building emotional intelligence is another critical aspect of managing relationships effectively. Emotional intelligence, the ability to understand and manage your own emotions and those of others, is deeply intertwined with critical thinking. It involves a high level of self-awareness, the ability to self-regulate, and the capacity for empathy and perspective-taking. For example, consider a scenario where your partner is upset about something you said. Instead of reacting defensively, use your emotional intelligence to consider their feelings and perspective. Why were they hurt by your comment? Could you have phrased it differently? This kind of empathy helps resolve the immediate conflict and strengthens the relationship in the long run, as it shows you care and respect the other person's feelings and viewpoints.

To bring these concepts to life, let's explore a few case scenarios that show critical thinking in action within relationship dynamics:

1. **Scenario 1**: Alex and Jordan are co-workers who often collaborate on projects. Jordan, who is more introverted, tends to communicate indirectly, hinting at issues rather than stating them outright. Alex, preferring direct communication, misses these cues and proceeds without addressing Jordan's concerns. This leads to frustration and inefficiency. By applying critical thinking, Alex could start paying closer attention to Jordan's cues and ask clarifying questions that help unveil any unspoken concerns, thereby improving their collaboration.
2. **Scenario 2**: Sam and Chris are in a long-term relationship and are discussing their future. Sam wants to move abroad for a job opportunity, while Chris prefers to stay close to family. Instead of this turning into a heated argument, they use critical thinking to analyze their priorities and fears associated with each option. They list the pros and cons of each choice and consider each other's perspectives deeply, which helps them arrive at a compromise that considers both their needs.
3. **Scenario 3**: Lee and Morgan, friends for years, find themselves in a conflict after a

misunderstanding at a social event where Lee felt ignored by Morgan. Instead of letting resentment build, Lee decides to address the issue directly. Using active listening, Lee expresses feelings without placing blame, allowing Morgan to explain the situation from a different perspective. This open communication clears up the misunderstanding and reinforces the strength of their friendship.

Each of these scenarios illustrates how critical thinking can transform potential conflicts into opportunities for strengthening relationships. By understanding and adapting to different communication styles, actively listening, questioning assumptions, and building emotional intelligence, you equip yourself with the tools to navigate the complexities of human relationships. As you continue to develop these skills, remember that each interaction is an opportunity to practice and refine your approach, making every conversation a step toward richer, more meaningful relationships.

4.5 TEACHING CHILDREN TO THINK CRITICALLY

Raising a child in today's fast-paced world requires more than just providing love and security; it demands equipping them with the skills to think critically and navigate complexities with confidence. As a parent, one of your most impactful roles is nurturing your child's curiosity and critical thinking from a young age. This doesn't just prepare them for academic success; it sets a foundation for lifelong learning and problem-solving capabilities.

Fostering Curiosity

A child's innate curiosity is the perfect starting point for developing critical thinking skills. Encourage this curiosity by being responsive to their 'why' questions, no matter how trivial or repetitive they might seem. Additionally, you can turn the question back on your child, and ask them why, or how, something is the way it is. If your child asks why the sky is blue, and continues with follow-up questions, you could ask them, 'Why do you think the sky is blue?' Wait for their response, then give them the correct answer. This utilizes not only emotional intelligence and active listening, but encourages their own critical thinking skills. Each question they ask is an opportunity to explore answers together, fostering a learning environment where questioning is valued. You can stimulate their curiosity further by turning daily routines into mini-exploration sessions. For example, a walk in the park can transform into a nature scavenger hunt, where you both look for specific types of leaves, bugs, or birds. Discussing why certain trees lose leaves at specific times of the year or why some insects are attracted to certain plants can spark interest and encourage deeper thinking about the natural world.

Another way to promote curiosity is through books. Choose stories that end with open-ended questions or scenarios that invite speculation and deduction. Discuss these endings with your child, asking what they think might happen next and why. This improves their ability to hypothesize and reason and makes reading an interactive and intellectually stimulating experience.

Critical Thinking in Education

Supporting your child's critical thinking development extends into their educational experiences. Engage regularly with your child's teachers to understand what they are learning and how it's being taught. This insight allows you to complement their schoolwork with at-home activities that reinforce critical thinking. For instance, if your child is learning about the water cycle at school, you can conduct simple experiments at home, like creating condensation with hot water and a cold plate, to visually demonstrate these concepts.

Encourage your child to discuss and debate topics covered in school, providing a safe space where they can express their thoughts and challenge ideas. This practice enhances their understanding and builds confidence in their reasoning abilities. It's important to teach them how to make connections between different subjects. Show them how math skills can help solve everyday problems, or how knowledge of history can provide insights into current events, reinforcing that learning is not just about memorizing facts but about understanding and applying knowledge.

Games and Activities

Integrating games that promote critical thinking into your child's playtime is both fun and educational. Games like chess, puzzles, and strategy-based board games encourage forward-thinking, strategic planning, and problem-solving. Even simple games like 'I Spy' or '20 Questions' can enhance critical observation and deductive reasoning skills. Make these games a regular part of family time, emphasizing the fun of thinking critically rather than treating it as a serious exercise.

You can also use technology to your advantage by choosing apps and video games that build critical skills. Look for ones that require problem-solving, planning, and decision-making, ensuring that screen time is both educational and engaging. However, balance this with plenty of hands-on activities that require physical interaction and real-world problem-solving.

Modeling Critical Thinking

Remember, children learn a lot by observation. Demonstrating your own critical thinking in everyday decisions shows them how to apply it in real life. Talk through your thought process aloud when making decisions, whether it's choosing a product based on consumer reviews or planning a family outing with consideration to weather and everyone's preferences. This visibility helps them understand how to approach decisions systematically and thoughtfully.

When faced with challenges or problems, model calmness and a methodical approach to solving them. Show that it's okay not to have all the answers and involve them in finding solutions. This not only improves their problem-solving skills but also teaches resilience and adaptability.

By incorporating these strategies—fostering curiosity, integrating critical thinking into education, engaging in thought-provoking games, and modeling critical thinking behaviors—you equip your child with the tools to think clearly and critically. These skills will serve them well beyond their school years into adulthood, helping them navigate the complexities of life with confidence and insight.

As we wrap up this chapter on enhancing personal decision-making through critical thinking, we've explored various aspects of financial planning, health, relationships, and children. Each section has provided strategies to apply critical thinking to improve your everyday life decisions. These tools solve immediate problems and prepare you for future challenges, ensuring that you and your family can face whatever comes your way with confidence and clarity. Moving forward, the next chapter will delve into professional settings, where we'll explore how critical thinking is essential in navigating workplace dynamics and making strategic career decisions.

Action Steps:

- **Conduct a Personal SWOT Analysis:** Identify a major decision you are currently facing, such as a career move or buying a home. Create a SWOT (Strengths, Weaknesses, Opportunities, Threats) analysis chart.
- **Practice Daily Expense Tracking:** Start a daily habit of recording all your expenses for one month. Categorize them into essentials (like rent, groceries, and utilities) and non-essentials (like dining out and entertainment). At the end of the month, review your spending patterns to identify areas where you can cut back or adjust your budget.
- **Engage in Critical Health Information Evaluation:** Next time you come across a new

health trend or diet plan, take a moment to evaluate its credibility. Check the source of the information, look for references to scientific studies, and consider the author's credentials.
- **Play Strategic Thinking Games:** Incorporate games that enhance critical thinking into your leisure time. Games like chess, puzzles, and strategy-based board games promote forward-thinking, planning, and problem-solving.

CHAPTER 5
WISDOM IN THE WORKPLACE

Imagine you're at the helm of a ship navigating through foggy waters. Every decision you make, from adjusting the sails to plotting the course, impacts not only your journey but also the crew relying on your leadership. In the professional realm, much like being the captain of a ship, every decision you make can have significant implications for your career and the people you work with. This chapter is about arming you with the strategies you need to make these decisions not just confidently but wisely, transforming potential workplace challenges into opportunities for growth and success.

5.1 STRATEGIC DECISION MAKING: A GUIDE FOR PROFESSIONALS

Frameworks for Decision-Making

In the complex world of business, strategic decision-making is not about following a set path, but rather about navigating through uncharted waters, making the right calls at the right times. Advanced decision-making frameworks are your compass and map in this process, providing structured methods that help you see beyond the immediate pressures to the broader horizons of business strategy.

One such framework is the **Balanced Scorecard**, which helps you view your organization from four essential perspectives:

- Financial
- Customer
- Internal Business Processes
- Learning and Growth

This framework ensures that your strategic decisions are balanced and aligned with the organization's long-term goals rather than being overly swayed by short-term gains or pressures.

Example of a Balanced Scorecard

Perspective	Objective	KPI	Target	Action Plan
Financial	Increase revenue	Annual Revenue Growth	10% increase	Launch new products, expand sales
	Improve cost efficiency	Operating cost reduction	5% decrease	Implement cost saving measures
Customer	Enhance customer satisfaction	Customer satisfaction score	15% improvement	Improve customer service training
	Increase customer retention	Customer retention rate	10% increase	Develop loyalty programs
Internal Business Processes	Optimize order fulfillment	Order fulfillment time	20% reduction	Streamline supply chain processes
	Improve process quality	Defect rate	30% reduction	Implement quality control systems
Learning and Growth	Develop employee skills	Training hours per employee	20% increase	Expand training programs
	Enhance employee satisfaction	Employee satisfaction score	10% improvement	Conduct regular feedback survey

Another powerful tool is the **Decision Matrix Analysis**, which allows you to evaluate and prioritize a list of options based on several predetermined criteria.

To use a Decision Matrix Analysis, start by listing all the options to be evaluated. Next, establish the criteria that are important for making the decision. These criteria should be relevant to the goals and objectives of the decision-making process. Assign a weight to each criterion based on its importance. This weight can be a simple scale, such as 1 to 5, where 5 indicates the highest importance. Once the criteria and their weights are determined, score each option against each criterion, usually on a scale of 1 to 10, where 10 indicates the best performance. Multiply each score by the weight of the corresponding criterion to get a weighted score for each criterion and sum these weighted scores for each option. The option with the highest total weighted score is typically the best choice.

This method is particularly useful when decisions involve multiple factors and potential outcomes that need to be weighed systematically. For example, when deciding on a new market to enter, factors like market size, competition, cost of entry, and potential ROI can be evaluated and scored in the matrix to determine the most viable option.

Analyzing Risks and Opportunities

Understanding the risks and opportunities associated with each decision is crucial. Risk analysis involves identifying potential negative outcomes and assessing their likelihood and impact. This might mean considering the financial loss if a new product fails or the impact on employee morale from canceling a paid holiday to cut costs. Conversely, opportunity analysis requires you to identify and evaluate potential benefits and explore how they can be maximized. It's about asking, "What can we gain from this decision?" and "How can we increase our chances of success?"

A practical method for performing this analysis is the SWOT (Strengths, Weaknesses, Opportunities, Threats) analysis, which we shared in the last chapter and used heavily in the professional space.

Case Studies

To illustrate these concepts, let's consider a few real-world applications of strategic decision-making:

- **Tech Startup Expansion**: A tech startup is considering expanding its service offerings. Using the Balanced Scorecard, the leadership team evaluates the potential financial returns and how the expansion aligns with customer needs and the company's capacity to innovate. They conduct a SWOT analysis to weigh the risks of spreading resources too thin against the opportunity to capture a larger market share.
- **Manufacturing Process Optimization**: A manufacturing company is looking to optimize its production processes. By applying the Decision Matrix Analysis, the management assesses various technology solutions based on criteria such as cost, implementation time, ROI, and potential to improve quality. This structured evaluation guides them to make a decision that balances short-term impacts with long-term benefits.

Incorporating Stakeholder Perspectives

Every strategic decision in a business setting affects, and is affected by, various stakeholders—employees, customers, investors, and even the community. Considering these different perspectives not only strengthens the decision-making process but also enhances acceptance of that decision and reduces chances for conflict after it is made.

Engaging stakeholders through surveys, meetings, or focus groups can provide valuable insights into their priorities and concerns. For instance, before rolling out a new employee performance evaluation system, gathering input from the staff might reveal potential resistance or suggestions for improvement that could make the system more effective and accepted.

By applying these advanced frameworks, methods, and considerations, your strategic decision-making process becomes not just a pathway to solving problems but a strategic lever for driving business success and growth. Whether you're steering a startup towards new markets, or guiding an international business through organizational changes, the ability to make informed, balanced, and strategic decisions is what defines true leadership in the workplace.

As you continue to navigate through this chapter, keep in mind that each decision you make is a building block in the architecture of your career and your organization. With the right tools and strategies, you're not just making choices; you're crafting a legacy of wisdom and success in the professional world.

5.2 CRITICAL THINKING FOR EFFECTIVE LEADERSHIP AND MANAGEMENT

In the realm of leadership and management, the ability to think critically isn't just an asset; it's a cornerstone upon which effective decision-making and problem-solving are built. Consider yourself in a leadership role during a stressful situation; your decisions don't just determine your course of action but are essential for the well-being and motivation of your team. Similarly, in a corporate setting, these leaders are equipped with sharp critical thinking skills to better navigate the challenges of a modern business environment. They use these analytical abilities to ensure their organizations' growth and foster a workplace climate of innovation and resilience.

Leadership and Critical Thinking

Understanding the integral role of critical thinking in leadership involves more than recognizing problems and solving them. It's about questioning conventional wisdom, challenging the status quo, and looking beyond the obvious to anticipate potential future issues. Critical thinkers in leadership roles evaluate all angles of a situation, including potential risks and benefits, to make informed decisions that align with long-term strategic goals. They are adept at interpreting data, questioning its validity, and integrating this information to guide their teams and organizations. This skill set enables leaders to not just react to the world as it is, but to envision and shape the future.

Take, for example, a leader considering the adoption of a new technology. The critical-thinking leader evaluates not only the immediate benefits and costs but also delves into how this technology could reshape the competitive landscape, affect employee workflows, or alter customer experiences. They might conduct scenario planning to anticipate various outcomes and develop contingency plans. This thorough analysis ensures that decisions are both proactive and strategic, rather than merely reactive or based on surface-level data.

Communicating with Clarity and Persuasion

Effective communication is another domain where critical thinking plays a pivotal role. Leaders must often distill complex information into clear, understandable messages that can persuade and motivate their teams. This requires a deep understanding of the subject at hand and an awareness of the audience's knowledge and beliefs. Critical thinkers are particularly good at this.

For instance, when presenting a new business strategy, a leader adept in critical thinking and communication might use analogies or relevant case studies to illustrate their points, making complex ideas more relatable and easier to grasp. They would also be prepared to provide evidence to back up their claims and to address counterarguments thoughtfully and respectfully, thereby enhancing their credibility and persuasiveness.

Developing a Vision

Developing a clear and compelling vision is perhaps one of the most strategic uses of critical thinking in leadership. A vision isn't just a lofty idea of what an organization might achieve in the future; it's a carefully crafted beacon that guides decision-making and strategy. It provides a framework within which critical decisions are made, ensuring consistency and alignment with the organization's goals and values.

Creating a vision for a company involves several key steps such as:

1. **Identify Core Values and Purpose.** Define the fundamental beliefs and purpose of the company.
2. **Analyze the Market and Competitors.** Understand the industry landscape, including market trends and competitors.
3. **Engage Stakeholders.** To gather diverse perspectives, involve key stakeholders, including employees, customers, and partners.
4. **Draft the Vision Statement.** Create a draft that articulates the long-term aspirations and goals of the company.
5. **Refine and Communicate.** Refine the vision statement based on feedback and ensure it is clearly communicated to all stakeholders.

Empowering Others

Finally, one of the most significant impacts of critical thinking in leadership is the ability to empower others. Leaders who think critically understand the importance of fostering these skills within their teams. They create environments where questioning and exploration are encouraged, team members feel safe expressing dissenting opinions, and rigorous debate leads to better solutions.

One effective strategy for fostering critical thinking among employees is the Socratic method. This method involves leaders asking probing questions that encourage deeper analysis and reflection. Instead of providing answers, these leaders guide their teams to find solutions through questioning and exploration. This helps develop the team's critical thinking skills and promotes a more collaborative and innovative workplace culture.

In these ways, critical thinking transforms leadership from a mere role to a dynamic capability that propels organizations forward. Leaders who harness these skills navigate their teams through uncertainties and complexities with greater agility and vision, ensuring sustained growth and success in today's fast-changing business landscape. As we move forward, consider how these strategies can be applied to improve individual leadership practices and enhance the collective wisdom of entire organizations.

5.3 FOSTERING A CULTURE OF CRITICAL THINKING IN TEAMS

Creating a team culture that values and actively promotes critical thinking is similar to cultivating a garden that encourages every plant to thrive and contribute to the ecosystem. It's about nurturing an environment where each team member feels empowered to ask questions, challenge norms, and offer unique perspectives without fear of ridicule or repercussions. Achieving such a culture begins with leadership but must permeate through every layer of an organization.

To build this kind of culture, start with transparency. Openness in processes and decision-making builds trust and invites team members to engage critically with the tasks at hand. For instance, when a project starts, sharing its goals, potential challenges, and success metrics openly sets the stage for inclusive and critical engagement. It encourages team members to ask questions and contribute ideas from the get-go, fostering a collaborative atmosphere.

Another effective strategy is facilitating regular brainstorming sessions that are structured yet open-ended. These sessions should encourage all participants to voice their thoughts equally, with ideas welcomed without immediate judgment or criticism. Techniques such as 'brainwriting,' where individuals write down ideas anonymously, can be particularly effective in drawing out thoughts from team members who might normally be hesitant to speak up in meetings. This method not only democratizes the process of idea generation but also ensures that a diverse range of ideas is heard, which can lead to innovative solutions and strategies.

Encouraging a culture of feedback is also critical. Constructive feedback mechanisms allow team members to reflect on their thought processes and decision-making frameworks. It's about creating a feedback loop that is not just top-down but lateral, allowing peers to learn from each other. Implementing regular peer-to-peer review sessions where team members can discuss recent decisions or projects can provide valuable insights and foster a continuous learning environment. These sessions help individuals understand different ways of thinking and approaching problems, which can broaden their own cognitive abilities.

Encouraging Diversity of Thought

The importance of diversity of thought in a team cannot be overstated. It brings different perspectives and experiences into the room, enriching the decision-making process and enhancing creativity and problem-solving. To cultivate this diversity, assembling teams from varied backgrounds, disciplines, and cultures is crucial. It means going beyond the traditional metrics of diversity to include diversity of experience, education, and thought.

However, having a diverse team is not enough if the full spectrum of ideas and opinions isn't heard. Leaders must actively encourage and sometimes mediate to ensure all voices are valued equally. This might involve training on unconscious biases, which can hinder how certain ideas or contributions are perceived. Workshops that highlight the importance of different perspectives and the benefits of inclusive dialogue can also be beneficial.

One practical approach is to assign 'devil's advocates' in meetings to ensure that multiple sides of an issue are explored. This role rotation not only encourages critical thinking but also prevents the stagnation of ideas, ensuring that the team does not fall into the trap of conformity, where the desire for harmony or conformity results in irrational or dysfunctional decision-making processes.

Collaborative Problem Solving

Effective, critical thinking-driven problem-solving sessions are the engines of innovation within a team. These sessions should be structured to maximize collective intelligence while minimizing the common pitfalls of collaborative efforts, such as dominance by more vocal members. Employing structured problem-solving techniques such as the **Six Thinking Hats**. This is a method for group discussion and individual thinking. It involves using six metaphorical hats of different colors, each representing a different style of thinking:

- **White Hat:** Focuses on facts, data, and information available or needed.
- **Red Hat:** Emphasizes emotions, intuitions, and feelings without justification.
- **Black Hat:** Looks at the negative aspects—caution, risks, and weaknesses.
- **Yellow Hat:** Considers optimism, benefits, and positive outcomes.

- **Green Hat:** Encourages creativity, new ideas, and alternative solutions.
- **Blue Hat:** Manages the thinking process, sets objectives, and organizes discussions.

This structured approach helps teams and individuals explore issues from multiple perspectives, improve decision-making, and foster creativity by consciously directing and balancing different modes of thinking.

Moreover, leveraging technology can enhance collaborative problem-solving. Tools that allow for real-time collaboration and idea-sharing can help gather input from team members regardless of their physical location. Platforms that support anonymity can also be useful in ensuring that ideas are judged on their merits rather than the stature of their proposer, encouraging a more honest and productive dialogue.

Measuring and Rewarding Critical Thinking

Recognizing and rewarding critical thinking in team settings can be challenging, primarily because it's an intangible skill. However, developing metrics that can indirectly measure critical thinking outcomes, such as the number of viable solutions generated during problem-solving sessions or the improvement in project outcomes due to innovative strategies, can be a start. While not perfect, these metrics can offer a tangible way to assess the impact of critical thinking on team performance.

Incentives don't always have to be monetary. Recognizing contributions during team meetings, featuring 'critical thinker of the month' in company newsletters, or providing opportunities for further education and professional development can also motivate team members to hone their critical thinking skills. The key is to align rewards with the organization's values and goals, ensuring that they reinforce the desired culture of critical thinking and continuous improvement.

By embedding these strategies into the fabric of your team's operations, you foster a culture that breathes critical thinking and paves the way for a more dynamic, innovative, and effective organizational environment. As teams become more adept at critical thinking, the organization as a whole becomes more capable of navigating the complexities and challenges of the modern business landscape, ensuring sustained growth and success.

5.4 NAVIGATING WORKPLACE CONFLICTS THROUGH CRITICAL ANALYSIS

In any professional environment, conflicts are as inevitable as deadlines. They can arise from misunderstandings, differences in values or objectives, or simply from the stress of daily pressures. But not all conflicts need to lead to negative outcomes. With the right approach, they can be transformed into opportunities for growth and innovation. Critical thinking plays an indispensable role in this transformation, allowing you to dissect the underlying issues and navigate through the emotional fog that often accompanies disagreements.

Understanding the dynamics of workplace conflicts starts with recognizing that conflict is not inherently bad. It often signals a diversity of ideas and perspectives, which is vital for organizational health. The key is to manage these conflicts constructively. When a conflict arises, step back and analyze the situation critically. Identify the root cause of the disagreement—is it a lack of resources, clashing personalities, differing priorities, or perhaps a combination of these factors? Once you understand the underlying issues, you can address them more effectively, rather than just dealing with the symptoms. For example, if a conflict stems from a lack of clarity in roles, the solution might involve revisiting job descriptions and responsibilities to ensure everyone is clear about their duties and expectations.

Moving forward to strategies for resolution, integrating critical thinking into your approach can significantly enhance the effectiveness of conflict management. Techniques such as negotiation and mediation are particularly useful.

Negotiation involves direct communication between the parties in conflict, aiming to reach an agreement that satisfies all involved. Here, critical thinking helps by enabling you to consider various negotiation strategies, anticipate the other party's needs and objections, and craft proposals that offer mutual benefits.

Mediation, on the other hand, involves a neutral third party to facilitate a resolution. In this scenario, a critical thinker can serve as an effective mediator by objectively analyzing the arguments from all sides, guiding the discussion in a constructive direction, and helping to find a middle ground.

The role of emotional intelligence in managing and resolving conflicts cannot be stressed enough. Emotional intelligence involves understanding and managing your own emotions, as well as empathizing with others. In conflict situations, high emotional intelligence allows you to keep your emotions from clouding judgment, maintain professionalism, and communicate effectively. It also helps you to understand the emotional underpinnings of the other party's perspective, which can be crucial for resolving the conflict amicably. For instance, recognizing that a colleague's hostility might stem from stress or insecurity rather than personal animosity can lead to a more empathetic and productive dialogue.

Lastly, let's consider preventative measures. Many conflicts can be avoided with clear communication and well-set expectations from the start. Regular team meetings and open lines of communication are fundamental in ensuring everyone is on the same page. Setting clear expectations regarding roles, outcomes, and behaviors helps prevent misunderstandings that can escalate into conflicts. Additionally, creating an organizational culture that values feedback and continuous improvement can encourage team members to express concerns early, before they grow into bigger issues. For example, implementing a system where employees can provide anonymous feedback might reveal potential problems early on, allowing management to address them proactively.

Incorporating these elements into your conflict management strategy not only helps in resolving disputes when they arise, but also minimizes the occurrence of conflicts in the first place. By fostering an environment where challenges are met with critical analysis, empathy, and clear communication, you can transform potential conflicts into opportunities for strengthening teamwork and enhancing organizational unity. As you continue to apply these principles, you'll likely discover that the skills you develop are not just useful in handling conflicts, but are essential tools for broader leadership and management effectiveness. This enhances both your professional relationships and the overall productivity of your team.

5.5 THE FUTURE OF WORK: CRITICAL THINKING SKILLS FOR THE NEW ECONOMY

In a world where change is the only constant, the future of work looks strikingly different from the present. The evolution of the workplace is propelled not only by technological advancements, but also by the global economy's complex demands. These changes necessitate a new kind of agility and foresight in the workforce. Critical thinking, a skill once reserved for leaders and innovators, is now becoming indispensable for professionals across all levels and industries. As we peer into the future, it becomes clear that skills such as adaptability, problem-solving, and innovation will not only become more valuable but essential for survival and success in the new economy.

Adaptability, in particular, stands out as a critical skill in an era where professional roles and industries are evolving rapidly. The ability to pivot and embrace new methods, technologies, and perspectives is crucial. For instance, consider the rise of remote work; professionals who adapt quickly to this model can maintain or even increase their productivity. Moreover, problem-solving skills are increasingly in demand as businesses face complex challenges that require innovative solutions. These aren't just technical problems but also strategic ones, where the ability to think critically and evaluate various scenarios and outcomes can set a professional apart from their peers.

Innovation, driven by critical thinking, is another key talent in the future of work. As businesses strive to stay relevant and competitive, the ability to adapt to new technologies and drive innovation becomes crucial. This means not just understanding existing technologies but imagining new uses for them. It involves a mindset that questions the status quo and looks for opportunities to improve, enhance, or even revolutionize current practices.

The impact of technological advancements such as artificial intelligence (AI) and automation on the workforce cannot be overstated. While some view these technologies as a threat to employment, they also present significant opportunities for those prepared to leverage these tools. Critical thinking skills are essential here, as they enable professionals to interface effectively with technology, utilizing it to optimize workflows, enhance decision-making processes, and create value. Moreover, as AI and automation take over routine tasks, the human workforce's role will likely shift towards more complex, strategic functions where critical thinking is irreplaceable.

Preparing for this uncertain future requires a proactive approach. It involves continuously scanning the horizon for emerging trends and technologies to allow an evaluation of their potential impact on your career and industry. This proactive planning isn't about having all the answers but about developing a keen sense of inquiry and preparedness. For example, staying informed through continuous learning and being open to new experiences can provide a significant advantage. Networking within and beyond your industry can also offer insights and opportunities that might not be apparent from the inside.

Moreover, the importance of lifelong learning and adaptability in professional development cannot be emphasized enough. The concept of a career has shifted from a linear trajectory to a more dynamic path where learning new skills and adapting to new roles becomes necessary for advancement. This shift makes continuous learning—whether through formal education, self-directed learning, or professional development activities—an integral part of career planning. It ensures that your skills and knowledge remain relevant and competitive.

As we wrap up this exploration of the critical thinking skills necessary for thriving in the new economy, remember that the landscape of work is continuously evolving. The ability to think **critically**, adapt **swiftly**, and innovate **consistently** are becoming the pillars upon which professional success is built. Looking ahead, these skills will not only help you navigate the complexities of the future workplace but also enable you to lead with confidence and insight in an increasingly unpredictable world.

Action Steps:

- **Start Using a Decision-Making Framework:** Begin by incorporating the Decision Matrix Analysis into your daily decision-making processes.
- **Engage in Critical Thinking Exercises:** Set aside time each week to engage in critical thinking exercises, such as brainstorming sessions or scenario planning.
- **Solicit and Give Constructive Feedback:** Foster a culture of feedback within your professional life, encouraging peers to share their thoughts on projects and decisions, and be open to receiving their insights.

CONGRATULATIONS ON REACHING THIS MILESTONE!

As you pause to reflect on the insights and exercises you've tackled so far, take a moment to acknowledge the progress you've made. Each chapter you've completed has been a step forward in sharpening your logical faculties and developing a sharper, more analytical mindset. Your dedication to this journey is impressive, and the skills you're building are valuable assets that will serve you well in countless aspects of your life.

To make the most of your progress and to ensure that you're on the right track, we'd love to hear from you! Your feedback is incredibly valuable, not just for you, but for future readers who will benefit from your experiences and insights.

Here are a few questions to guide your review:

1. **Which chapters or exercises have resonated with you the most?** What aspects of the book have been particularly helpful or enlightening in your journey so far?
2. **Have you encountered any challenges or "aha" moments?** Sharing specific instances where you struggled or experienced breakthroughs can be incredibly valuable.
3. **How has your approach to critical thinking evolved?** Are there any new strategies or perspectives you've adopted that have made a difference in your decision-making process?

For your convenience, you can scan this QR code which will take you directly to our review page

Once again, congratulations on your progress! Keep up the fantastic work as you continue to explore and apply the principles of critical thinking. We're excited for you to discover the many benefits that lie ahead in the remaining chapters.

CHAPTER 6
PRACTICAL EXERCISES FOR EVERYDAY THOUGHT

Every day life can feel like a day in a circus—constantly spinning plates and juggling balls, trying to keep everything moving and in sync. That's essentially what your brain is trying to do every day, consistently maintaining a myriad of thoughts, decisions, and problems in the air, waiting to pull something useful. Developing everyday practices for critical thinking won't lessen your workload but can make you more adept at handling it; it doesn't decrease the number of balls you're juggling, but it makes you into an expert everyday problem solver by embedding critical thinking into your daily routines. Let's dive into some practical exercises that you can incorporate into your everyday life to sharpen your cognitive abilities and enhance your decision-making prowess.

6.1 DAILY HABITS TO ENHANCE YOUR CRITICAL THINKING

Morning Questions

Kickstart your day not just with a cup of coffee but with a stimulating mental routine. Each morning, challenge yourself with a set of questions that probe your anticipated schedule or routine decisions. For example, ask yourself, "What are the three most critical tasks I need to accomplish today, and why are they important?" or "What could be potential stumbling blocks, and how might I overcome them?" This exercise sets a purposeful tone for your day, encouraging you to approach daily activities with intention and foresight. It's about anticipating challenges and strategizing solutions in advance, making you more prepared and proactive in tackling your day.

Critical Reading

Dedicate a part of your day to reading a variety of sources critically. This means you can skip all the dense academic journals (unless that's your cup of tea). Instead, mix it up with articles from trusted news sources, blogs, and even forums, focusing on a diverse range of topics. As you read, actively analyze the content by noting biases, strengths, and weaknesses in the arguments presented. Ask yourself, "What is the author's main point? What evidence supports this argument? Is there a clear bias, and how does it affect the message?" This practice not only enhances your understanding of different viewpoints but also sharpens your ability to evaluate information critically, a skill that's invaluable in both personal and professional contexts.

Problem-Solving Routine

Integrate a daily practice of solving puzzles or problems that require logical reasoning and creative thinking. This could be anything from Sudoku and crosswords to more complex logic puzzles available in apps and online platforms. The key is challenging your brain with tasks requiring thinking outside the box and applying logical strategies. Over time, this routine improves your problem-solving skills and enhances your ability to think under pressure, a highly beneficial quality in navigating everyday life.

Decision Review

End your day by reflecting on a decision you made, evaluating both the process and the outcome. Consider a decision that significantly impacted your day: perhaps you decided to delegate a task at work, chose a new recipe for dinner, or negotiated a deal on a purchase. Reflect on how you arrived at that decision:

- What factors did you consider?
- Were there any biases that influenced your choice?
- How did the outcome align with your expectations?

This reflection helps you understand your decision-making process and encourages you to learn from your experiences, continually refining your thinking and decision-making skills.

By incorporating these exercises into your daily routine, you transform every day into an opportunity for cognitive growth and development. These practices, though simple, are powerful tools for enhancing your ability to think critically and make informed decisions. As you move through your day, from the moment you wake up to when you wind down, remember that each activity and decision is a chance to exercise and expand your mental capabilities. So, go ahead and challenge yourself—turn your daily routines into stepping stones for cognitive excellence and watch as your day-to-day life not only becomes more managed but also more enriched.

6.2 REAL-WORLD SCENARIOS: WHAT WOULD YOU DO?

Navigating through life's complicated challenges often feels like being a character in an elaborate role-playing game where each decision can take you down a drastically different path. In this section, we're going to plunge into various real-world scenarios you might encounter in your daily life—at work, during a casual social gathering, or when facing an ethical dilemma. The aim is not just to decide but to dissect the decision-making process, play around with different perspectives, predict outcomes, and learn how to refine your critical thinking skills through feedback.

Scenario Analysis

Consider a work-related scenario: You're a project manager, and your team is facing a tight deadline. You discover that a key piece of work submitted by a team member needs to be revised to the required standard. The easy route? Redo the work yourself to ensure quality and meet the deadline. However, let's analyze this.

- What are the long-term ramifications of this decision?
- Will it set a precedent for the team member's future contributions?
- Could it affect the morale or the learning curve of the team?

Here, critical thinking nudges you to consider not just the immediate impact of your decision on the project's timeline but also its long-term effects on team dynamics and individual growth. By weighing these factors, you might decide instead to have a constructive feedback session with the team member, offering guidance to redo the work, which supports their professional development and reinforces the needed standard of quality.

Role-Playing

Next, let's shift to a social scenario. Imagine you're at a family gathering where a heated debate about a political issue breaks out. You have your strong views, but so does everyone else at the table. Here, role-playing different perspectives can be enlightening. Try stepping into the shoes of someone who disagrees with you. Why might they feel the way they do? What experiences or information have shaped their views? Engaging in this mental exercise doesn't mean you have to change your stance. Instead, it broadens your understanding of the issue and enhances your empathy for others' viewpoints. This practice can transform what might have been a tense argument into a more respectful and insightful discussion, where you come away with a richer understanding of the people you care about.

Outcome Prediction

Consider an ethical dilemma: Your company is offering a significant promotion, but you've heard through informal channels that your closest colleague, who might also be a contender, is going through some personal issues that could affect their performance. Applying for the promotion could potentially add to their stress. Here, the outcomes of different decisions are predicted. How will it impact your relationship with your colleague if you decide to use it? Could it motivate them, or would it strain your teamwork? Conversely, if you hold back, what might be the implications for your career? Are there ways to support your colleague's situation while still pursuing your professional goals? By predicting possible outcomes, you refine your ability to anticipate the consequences of your actions, which is a cornerstone of strategic thinking.

Feedback Loop

Finally, it's crucial to establish a feedback loop. Let's say you made a significant decision to switch careers. After some time in your new field, reach out for feedback. Talk to mentors, peers, and even yourself through self-reflection.

1. What has worked?
2. What hasn't?
3. What lessons have you learned?
4. How could you apply them moving forward?

This feedback loop is invaluable as it not only helps you gauge the effectiveness of your decision but also guides your future decisions. It's about continuously refining your decision-making process based on real-world outcomes and insights essential for personal and professional growth.

By engaging in these exercises, you not only enhance your problem-solving and decision-making skills but also deepen your understanding of yourself and how you interact with the world around you. Each scenario, each role-play, each prediction, and each feedback session builds your repertoire of skills, making you not just a thinker but a proficient doer in the vast landscape of everyday challenges.

6.3 ANALYZING NEWS ARTICLES: A CRITICAL THINKING EXERCISE

In a world swamped with information, being able to sift through news articles critically is more than a skill—it's a necessity. Think of yourself as a detective when you approach the news. Your goal? To unearth the truth and understand multiple facets of the story. To start, selecting a range of articles from diverse sources is crucial. This includes outlets that might align with your views and those that challenge them. The idea here is to expose yourself to a spectrum of perspectives, which can help mitigate the tunnel vision that often comes from consuming news from a single source. For instance, if you're exploring a political event, read multiple outlets with different sources. You might also look at international perspectives from reputable global news services, which can provide insights that domestic media might overlook. This variety broadens your understanding and sharpens your ability to compare and contrast different narratives.

Once you have selected your articles, the next step is identifying biases. News isn't always just about facts; it often includes the writer's or the publication's point of view. Start by examining the language used in the articles. Are there emotionally charged words that seem designed to elicit a strong reaction? Does the article use loaded terms that imply judgment? For example, describing a group as "freedom fighters" vs. "terrorists" can significantly influence the reader's perception. Also, look at what the article chooses to focus on or ignore. A report highlighting the economic benefits of a new policy while glossing over the social challenges presents a skewed perspective. Recognizing these biases isn't about discrediting the source but understanding the lens through which the story is told. This awareness is crucial in critically navigating through the information presented.

Cross-referencing facts is your next detective move. This process involves verifying the critical pieces of information presented in the article against other reputable sources. If an article claims, for instance, that a new study found a particular drug effective in treating a disease, don't take it at face value. Look up the study. Check at least three separate sources, such as academic journals or reputable medical websites, to see if the findings are presented accurately. Often, news articles simplify or cherry-pick data to fit the narrative, sometimes leading to misleading representations of research findings. By cross-referencing, you ensure that the information you rely on is not just a regurgitation of a potentially biased report but a verified fact.

Lastly, engage in critical discussions about the articles you've read. This could be with friends, a book club, or even online forums dedicated to critical thinking and news analysis. The goal here is to challenge your interpretations and open up to insights from others, which can reveal angles you might not have considered. When discussing, focus on presenting your understanding and rationale for your viewpoints rather than winning an argument. Ask open-ended questions like, "What do you think the implications of this policy might be?" or "Could there be an aspect we are missing?" These discussions can be enlightening, revealing the complexity of issues and the value of diverse viewpoints in enriching your understanding.

Incorporating these steps into your routine when engaging with news articles transforms a passive activity into an active investigation. You become not just a consumer of information but a critical thinker, capable of navigating the complexities of modern media landscapes with discernment and insight. As you continue to apply these strategies, they become second nature, equipping you with the tools to stay informed and insightful in an increasingly complicated world.

6.4 DEBATING ETHICAL DILEMMAS: SHARPENING YOUR ANALYTICAL SKILLS

Ethical dilemmas are a part of our daily lives, presenting situations where choices are not merely about right or wrong but involve a complex interplay of moral principles. Picture this: You're in a scenario where you must decide between telling a painful truth or a comforting lie, or perhaps you're at work, and you have to choose between whistleblowing on unethical practices or protecting your job. These aren't just hypotheticals; they are real choices that test our values and ethical compass. To navigate these dilemmas effectively, you need to understand and rigorously evaluate the moral principles at play.

Engaging with ethical dilemmas involves a structured approach to debating, which can be enlightening, whether conducted internally or within a group setting. Begin by clearly defining the dilemma and the moral principles it involves. For instance, if the dilemma is about whether to return a large sum of money you found, the principles could include honesty versus self-interest. Once the dilemma is set, explore each principle's implications. What are the consequences of following one principle over another? Who benefits, and who suffers? This kind of structured debate forces you to confront the complexities of ethical decision-making, making you more adept at handling such challenges in real life.

When justifying decisions made in these debates, it's crucial to base your arguments on established ethical theories or principles. This isn't just about stating what you would do but also explaining why based on ethical reasoning. For example, utilitarianism advocates for actions that maximize happiness for the most significant number of people to justify returning the money. Or, you might use Kantian ethics, which emphasizes duty and the categorical imperative, to argue why whistleblowing is not just a choice but a moral obligation. Articulating your reasoning in this way deepens your understanding of ethical frameworks and enhances your ability to communicate your ethical decisions clearly and convincingly.

Reflecting on personal values is another critical aspect of dealing with ethical dilemmas. It involves examining how your values align or conflict with the decisions you tend to make. Ask yourself, "What do my decisions say about what I value?" For instance, if you often find yourself prioritizing professional success over personal integrity, what does that reveal about your values? Are you comfortable with that alignment? This reflection isn't about judging your choices but understanding the values that drive them, which can be incredibly insightful. It allows you to realign your actions with your values or reconsider what you truly value, ensuring that your decisions reflect who you are and who you aspire to be.

Regularly engaging with ethical dilemmas through structured debate, decision justification, and reflection on personal values will equip you with the skills to make thoughtful, moral decisions. These activities prepare you to handle moral complexities in your personal and professional life and foster a deeper understanding of yourself and your ethical beliefs. As you continue to explore and apply these exercises, you'll find that your capacity for ethical reasoning and decision-making becomes more robust, making you a better thinker and a more honest and reflective individual.

6.5 REFLECTIVE JOURNALING FOR CRITICAL THINKERS

Reflective journaling is like having a personal coach locked within the pages of a notebook, one who is relentlessly honest and infinitely patient. Setting up a reflective journal dedicated to critical thinking exercises and daily reflections provides a structured space to dissect your thoughts and decisions, understand your cognitive biases, and track your growth over time. Start by choosing a journal that feels inviting and personal. This could be a classic notebook, a digital app, or even a series of documents on your computer. The key is consistency in use, so select a medium you'll likely use regularly.

Dedicate the first few pages to outlining your goals with this journal. Are you looking to enhance your decision-making skills, become more aware of your biases, or improve your problem-solving abilities? Having clear objectives will guide your entries and give you a metric against which to measure your progress. Next, create sections based on different areas you want to focus on. For instance, you might have a section for daily decisions, one for critical reading reflections, and another for personal bias observations. This organization not only keeps your journal tidy but also makes it easier to review specific aspects of your thinking when needed.

Structured reflections in your journal should focus on dissecting your analytical processes, pinpointing biases, and identifying areas for improvement. Each entry should follow a clear format:

- Describe the situation or decision.
- Analyze the thought process behind it.
- Identify any biases that might have influenced you.
- Conclude with what you learned and what you could improve.

For example, after a meeting where you made a significant decision, write about how you approached the decision, what factors you considered, what you might have overlooked, and how you feel about the outcome. This structured approach deepens your understanding of your thought patterns and reinforces the habit of critical self-reflection.

Progress Tracking

To effectively track your progress in developing critical thinking skills, setting specific, measurable milestones is essential. These could be as simple as increasing the frequency of your journal entries, tackling more complex decision-making scenarios each month, or reducing the influence of certain biases over time. Use your journal to assess your progress against these milestones regularly. Reflect on entries from months prior and compare them with recent ones to see if you can spot any trends or improvements. Are you asking deeper questions? Have your biases shifted? Are you making more informed decisions? Documenting these observations can provide motivational insights into your growth and encourage you to keep pushing your boundaries.

Moreover, consider setting up a self-assessment schedule—perhaps every three months—to formally review your progress. Use this review to adjust your goals and methods if necessary. Critical thinking is a dynamic process, and your journal should adapt to your evolving understanding.

Sharing Insights

One of the most enriching aspects of keeping a reflective journal is the opportunity to share and discuss your insights with others. This could be with peers, mentors, or even a personal blog audience. Sharing allows you to externalize your thoughts and receive feedback, providing new perspectives you might not have considered. It also holds you accountable for your growth and can be incredibly validating and motivating. Make it a point to share at least one insight or reflection from your journal each month. Whether it's discussing a recent bias you've observed in your decision-making or a particular success story where critical thinking saved the day, these discussions can significantly enhance your understanding and application of the concepts.

Engaging in reflective journaling transforms the abstract concept of 'improving critical thinking' into a tangible, actionable practice. Through daily entries, structured reflection, progress tracking, and sharing insights, this journal becomes more than just a collection of thoughts. It becomes a roadmap to personal and intellectual growth, charting a course through the complexities of your cognitive landscape and guiding you toward becoming a more thoughtful, informed, and discerning individual.

In closing, while today's chapter ends here, the journey of enhancing your critical thinking through reflective journaling is just beginning. Each page you fill is a step forward in deepening your understanding of yourself and honing your cognitive abilities. As you turn the page to the next chapter, remember that each reflection and insight is a building block in the foundation of a sharper, more critical mind.

Action Steps:

- **Start an everyday critical thinking journal, and use it every day for at least 30 days.**
- **Create an ethical dilemma, analyze the scenario, and role-play the opposite side.**
- **Analyse several news articles and find the sources and any conflicting information.**

CHAPTER 7
OVERCOMING OBSTACLES TO CRITICAL THINKING

The process of critical thinking can be similar to a maze: mental blocks and biases can often serve as barriers, complicating the path to clear, rational thoughts. In this chapter, we'll explore how to identify these barriers, understand their origins, and develop strategies to overcome them, ensuring a smoother journey toward better decision-making and problem-solving.

7.1 RECOGNIZING AND OVERCOMING MENTAL BLOCKS

Identification of Blocks

Mental blocks in critical thinking can be as subtle as they are debilitating. They often manifest in one or more of the following ways:

- **Cognitive Overload.** This is where the sheer volume of information paralyzes decision-making. It's like trying to find a needle in a haystack; the task seems impossible.
- **Fear of Failure.** Another standard block is the fear of failure, which can deter you from taking necessary risks or trying new approaches. It's like standing on the edge of a diving board, too terrified to jump.
- **Fixed Mindset.** Lastly, there's the fixed mindset, which locks you into a specific way of thinking, preventing growth and adaptation. It's as if you're wearing blinders, making it impossible to see the potential around you.

To start dismantling these blocks, begin by acknowledging their presence. Self-awareness is a powerful tool. Reflect on moments when you felt stuck, or your usual problem-solving strategies failed. What were the circumstances? Identifying patterns can help you anticipate and mitigate similar blocks in the future.

Strategies for Overcoming Blocks

Once you've identified your standard mental blocks, the next step is to develop strategies to overcome them. For cognitive overload, try breaking down tasks into manageable steps. This method, often called "chunking," simplifies complex information, making it easier to process and act upon.

If you're grappling with the fear of failure, consider implementing mindfulness exercises. Techniques like focused breathing or meditation can help reduce anxiety and boost your confidence in decision-making. These practices encourage a mental reset, giving you the clarity to approach problems with a fresh perspective.

For those stuck in a fixed mindset, actively seeking diverse perspectives can be transformative. Engage with people who challenge your viewpoints, or immerse yourself in environments different from your norm. This exposure can catalyze new ways of thinking, breaking the mold of your fixed mindset.

Mental Flexibility Exercises

Regularly engage with unfamiliar subjects or learn new skills to enhance your mental flexibility. This could be as simple as taking up a hobby outside your comfort zone or as structured as enrolling in a course unrelated to your field. These activities force your brain to forge new neural pathways, improving your ability to think laterally and solve problems creatively.

Building Resilience

Building resilience is crucial in overcoming mental blocks and enhancing your critical thinking skills. Resilience isn't about avoiding failure but learning to move forward despite setbacks. Expose yourself to challenging ideas and situations regularly. This could mean tackling complex projects at work or engaging in debates on topics where you're not the expert. Each challenge is an opportunity to strengthen your mental resilience, making you better equipped to handle future obstacles in your critical thinking journey.

By recognizing and actively addressing these mental blocks, you clear the path to more effective critical thinking and acquire new skills and techniques to navigate the stress and challenges of everyday life with greater agility and confidence. As you continue to implement these strategies and exercises, you'll find that what once seemed like insurmountable barriers will begin to diminish, leaving you with a clearer, more open pathway to knowledge and understanding.

7.2 DEALING WITH INFORMATION OVERLOAD: A SELECTIVE APPROACH

In today's digital age, you're bombarded with constant information, from social media updates and breaking news to lengthy emails and detailed reports. It's like standing under a waterfall, trying to catch water with your hands; grasping it all is impossible, no matter how hard you try. This relentless influx can lead to a sense of being overwhelmed, making it challenging to focus and make informed decisions. However, with the right strategies, you can navigate this flood of information effectively, ensuring you remain clear-headed and vigilant.

First, let's talk about efficiently navigating through vast amounts of information. The key here is to avoid trying and consuming everything but rather to become selective about what you pay attention to. Start by setting clear objectives for what you need from the information. Are you looking for data to support a business decision, insights for a personal project, or just staying updated on industry trends? Your goal will dictate your approach. For example, your objective is to stay informed about the latest technology trends. In that case, you might prioritize reading industry-specific blogs and reports and filter out unrelated news. This targeted approach saves time and keeps your cognitive load manageable, allowing you to focus on information that adds value to your objectives.

Now, onto prioritization techniques. Not all information is created equal, so it's crucial to prioritize based on relevance, credibility, and urgency. Develop a habit of quickly assessing the source of the information. Check the credibility by reviewing the author's credentials or the publication's reputation. Then, evaluate the relevance; does this information align with your current needs or objectives? Lastly, consider the urgency. Is this something that requires immediate attention, or can it wait? For instance, an email from a major client with a subject line indicating a pressing issue takes priority over a generic newsletter. You might find it helpful to use tools like email filters or news aggregators that can automatically categorize information based on these criteria, helping you focus on what's truly important.

Digesting information in phases is another effective strategy, especially when dealing with complex data or lengthy reports. Break down the information into manageable segments and allow time for reflection and analysis between each phase. This approach prevents cognitive overload and makes it easier to understand and retain the information. For example, if you're researching a new market for your business, you could divide your research into phases like market size, customer demographics, competitors, and regulatory environment. Tackle each segment separately, take notes, and reflect on what the data means for your business before moving on to the next segment. This phased approach makes the research process more digestible. It allows deeper insights to emerge as you connect the dots between different data segments.

Lastly, let's talk about tool utilization. Numerous tools and resources are available that can help you filter and organize information effectively. RSS feeds, for instance, can be customized to deliver news from preferred sources directly to you, cutting down on the time you spend searching for information. Project management tools like OneNote or Evernote can help you organize information related to specific projects, keeping all relevant data in one place and easily accessible. Additionally, consider using apps like Evernote or OneNote for note-taking and organizing information from various sources in a searchable, centralized location. These tools help manage information and ensure that you have access to this organized knowledge whenever you need to make decisions or solve problems.

By adopting these strategies, you transform the challenge of information overload into an opportunity for efficient learning and decision-making. With practice, using these techniques to sift through noise and irrelevant information will save you time and help you stay ahead in life and business.

7.3 THE FEAR OF BEING WRONG AND HOW TO CONQUER IT

One of the more paralyzing fears that throttle the pipeline of critical thinking is the dread of being incorrect. This fear isn't just about making a mistake; it's about what that mistake might signify about us to others and, more importantly, to ourselves. Psychologically, this fear is rooted deeply in our ego and self-identity. From a young age, many of us are conditioned to equate being right with being valued or successful. Therefore, the prospect of being wrong can often feel like a threat to our self-worth. This fear can be particularly stifling in competitive environments or where a high value is placed on precision and correctness, such as in many workplaces. The constant pressure to avoid mistakes can lead to a defensive mindset, where the primary goal is not necessarily to find the best solution or answer but rather to not be wrong. This defensive posture can severely hamper genuine learning and innovation, as both inherently involve some degree of trial and error.

Cultivating a growth mindset is a powerful antidote to the fear of being wrong. This concept, popularized by psychologist Carol Dweck, champions the idea that our abilities and intelligence can be developed through dedication and hard work. It's a perspective that thrives on challenges and sees failures not as evidence of unintelligence but as encouraging stepping stones for growth and stretching our existing abilities. With a growth mindset, you cherish learning and resilience, which are vital components of critical thinking. Embracing this mindset involves shifting how you view intelligence and mistakes. It means understanding that being wrong is an inevitable part of the learning process and not a reflection of your intellectual capacities. When you adopt this viewpoint, the fear of being wrong loses its grip, and you become more open to taking risks and experimenting, which are critical for developing strong critical thinking skills.

Creating safe spaces for making mistakes is another strategy that can help mitigate the fear of being wrong. This involves fostering environments—in both personal and professional settings—where mistakes are tolerated and viewed as opportunities for learning. For instance, some innovative companies hold 'failure forums' where employees can share mistakes and the lessons learned from them. These forums help to destigmatize failure and promote it as a valuable learning tool. In personal settings, this could involve surrounding yourself with friends or family who support your learning endeavors and respond to mistakes with encouragement rather than criticism. When people feel safe, they are more likely to take risks and engage in trial-and-error learning, which is essential for developing critical thinking.

Lastly, reframing mistakes is crucial. Instead of viewing them as failures, see them as integral steps towards understanding and mastery. This reframe can transform your approach to critical thinking and learning. When you make a mistake, instead of beating yourself up, ask yourself: What can I learn from this? What will I do differently next time? This approach not only alleviates the fear of being wrong but also turns every error into a stepping stone toward greater understanding and proficiency. For example, if you make an error in a project, instead of hiding it or dwelling on the mistake, analyze what went wrong, discuss it with colleagues or mentors, and use that knowledge to improve the project or to prevent similar mistakes in the future. This proactive approach to mistakes encourages a deeper engagement with your work. It fosters a more nuanced understanding of the issues at hand, which is essential for effective critical thinking.

Understanding the psychological roots of the fear of being wrong, cultivating a growth mindset, creating safe spaces for making mistakes, and reframing these mistakes as learning opportunities can significantly enhance your ability to think critically. These strategies transform the fear of being wrong from a paralyzing force into a constructive tool that encourages learning and innovation. As you continue implementing these approaches, you are more effective in problem-solving and decision-making and have become more resilient and adaptable.

7.4 BREAKING FREE FROM GROUPTHINK AND PEER PRESSURE

When you're in a meeting or part of a team project, have you ever noticed how sometimes a consensus is reached surprisingly quickly? It seems great on the surface—everyone agrees, so the decision must be the correct one, right? Not necessarily. This scenario can often be a classic case of groupthink. Groupthink occurs when the desire for harmony in a group leads to an irrational or dysfunctional decision-making outcome. It's like everyone has decided to swim in the same direction without really checking if there are sharks in the water. The signs of groupthink include the illusion of invulnerability, collective rationalization to discount warnings, and an unquestioned belief in the group's inherent morality. These symptoms can stifle individual creativity and critical thinking, leading to suboptimal outcomes.

To combat groupthink, fostering an environment encouraging dissent and diversity of thought is crucial. This can be achieved by promoting an open dialogue where all opinions are valued. As a leader or team member, you can initiate this by actively soliciting input from quieter members who might be hesitant to speak up. Pose questions like, "Does anyone see potential downsides to this approach?" or "I'd love to hear a different perspective." It's about creating a safe space where dissent is tolerated and seen as valuable. Another effective strategy is the role of a designated devil's advocate. Rotate this role among team members for different projects or meetings. The devil's advocate's job is to question assumptions and push back on ideas, providing a healthy counterbalance to the prevailing group opinion.

Maintaining personal integrity and the willingness to stand alone with one's convictions plays a pivotal role in overcoming the pressures of groupthink. It involves being true to your values and beliefs, even when they conflict with the group's ideas. This isn't about being adversarial; instead, it's about respectfully expressing your views and supporting them with clear, rational arguments. This can be challenging, especially in a strongly cohesive group where the pressure to conform can be intense. However, standing firm in your convictions contributes to better group decisions and earns you respect as a thinker who doesn't just go with the flow.

Leadership plays a decisive role in fostering groupthink or encouraging independent, critical thinking. Leaders set the tone for group dynamics. Leaders need to model the behaviors they want to see to cultivate a culture where critical thinking is valued over conformity. This includes showing openness to being wrong, actively seeking out alternative opinions, and publicly valuing contributions that challenge the status quo. Leaders should also be mindful of the dynamics that might promote groupthink, such as a rigid hierarchy or a too-cohesive group. Encouraging team members to engage in healthy debate and providing platforms for sharing diverse thoughts can mitigate these risks. For example, regular brainstorming sessions where all ideas are welcome and no immediate criticism is allowed can be an excellent way for team members to feel safe and encouraged to think independently.

By understanding and addressing groupthink, encouraging dissent, maintaining personal integrity, and shaping leadership practices to support these efforts, you empower yourself and others to break free from the confines of conformity. This enriches the decision-making process with many perspectives and critical evaluations and fosters a more dynamic, innovative, and effective team environment. As you continue to nurture these practices, remember that each step taken to challenge the norm is a stride toward better outcomes and a stronger, more resilient professional identity.

7.5 ENCOURAGING OPEN-MINDEDNESS AND CURIOSITY

Open-mindedness is like the lubricant for your brain's gears—it helps everything run smoother and more efficiently. Adopting an open-minded approach unlocks a higher level of critical thinking and paves the way for personal and intellectual growth. This isn't just about being receptive to different viewpoints; it's about actively seeking them out and considering them on their own merits, which can significantly deepen your understanding of complex issues and enhance your problem-solving skills.

Imagine for a moment that you're trying to solve a challenging problem at work. If you approach it with a closed mind, you will likely rely solely on tried and tested methods, which might not always be the best solution. Open-mindedness empowers you to explore innovative solutions, leading to more effective and creative outcomes. This flexibility can be a game-changer in today's fast-paced, ever-changing world. Moreover, being open-minded helps you build better professional and personal relationships, fostering a more inclusive and respectful environment. People are naturally drawn to those who value and respect their opinions, creating a positive feedback loop that encourages further sharing of ideas and perspectives.

Now, let's talk about curiosity, which is essentially the engine that drives open-mindedness. Curiosity pushes you to ask questions, seek new information, and explore unfamiliar territory. It compels you to look beyond your immediate understanding and consider alternative explanations and viewpoints. Think of curiosity as your personal detective—it doesn't rest until it uncovers the truth, no matter how deeply it's buried. By nurturing your curiosity, you enhance your ability to gather and analyze information and maintain a sense of excitement and engagement with the world around you. This relentless pursuit of knowledge not only makes life more exciting but also significantly enhances your critical thinking skills by constantly challenging you to reassess your understanding of the world.

To cultivate and maintain this sense of curiosity, consider engaging in exercises that push you out of your intellectual comfort zones, such as reading books on unfamiliar subjects or attending workshops in different fields. Physical or virtual travel can also be an excellent way to expose yourself to new cultures and ideas. Even something as simple as starting conversations with people from diverse backgrounds can broaden your horizons and challenge your preconceived notions. These activities encourage you to think in new and different ways, fostering open-mindedness and enhancing your problem-solving abilities.

Another crucial aspect of fostering open-mindedness is mitigating confirmation bias—the tendency to favor information that confirms your existing beliefs. This bias can be a significant barrier to open-minded thinking, as it closes you off to potentially valuable information and insights. To counteract this, consciously seek out and consider information that contradicts or challenges your views. This might involve following thought leaders with different perspectives or engaging with content from media outlets outside your usual preferences. Additionally, practicing devil's advocacy—arguing against your own beliefs—can be an effective way to expose any hidden biases and strengthen your capacity for critical thought.

By embracing open-mindedness and curiosity, you enhance your ability to think critically and open yourself up to a richer, more varied understanding of the world. These traits are invaluable for personal development and professional success in an increasingly complex and interconnected global landscape.

As we close this chapter, remember that the journey to enhancing your critical thinking skills is ongoing. The strategies and exercises discussed here are tools to help you navigate this path. By committing to fostering open-mindedness and curiosity, you equip yourself with the ability to continuously learn, adapt, and grow—qualities that are essential in today's ever-changing world. In the next chapter, we'll explore advanced strategies for making decisions that make sense—a crucial skill for anyone looking to apply their enhanced critical thinking abilities in practical, impactful ways.

Action Steps:

- **Write About Situational Blocks in Your Critical Thinking Journal:** Each evening, take 10 minutes to write about a situation from your day where you felt mentally stuck or overwhelmed. Note what caused the block, how you felt, and any patterns you noticed over time. This practice will help you become more aware of your mental blocks and how to address them.
- **Use The Pomodoro Technique for Complex Tasks:** When you have a big task, such as reading a detailed report or completing a challenging project, use the *Pomodoro Technique* to break it down. Set a timer for 25 minutes and focus on one part of the task. After the timer goes off, take a 5-minute break. Repeat this cycle four times, then take a longer break of 15-30 minutes. This method makes large tasks more manageable and keeps you focused.
- **Practice Reframing Mistakes:** Create a habit of reflecting on mistakes by setting aside 15 minutes each week to review any errors you made. Write down the mistake, why it happened, and what you learned. Then, reframe the error as a positive learning experience. This practice helps shift your mindset from fearing mistakes to viewing them as valuable learning opportunities, reducing the fear of being wrong.

CHAPTER 8
ADVANCED STRATEGIES: MAKING DECISIONS THAT MAKE SENSE

Each of our days is filled with choices, both small choices and life-changing ones. It's like going to a market or a mall—there are so many possible choices; where do you spend your hard-earned money? How do you sift through the noise and options to make a purchase you won't regret? In this chapter, we explore advanced decision-making strategies that equip you to navigate the marketplaces of your life—be they literal or metaphorical.

8.1 THE SOCRATIC METHOD: ANCIENT TECHNIQUES FOR MODERN PROBLEMS

Dialogue as a Tool

The Socratic Method, a form of cooperative argumentative dialogue used by Socrates, is famed for probing moral and ethical issues. At its core, this method is about challenging assumptions through disciplined questioning, making it an invaluable tool in the critical thinker's arsenal. Think of it as peeling an onion, layer by layer, to uncover the core of the truth. We previously took a glance at the Socratic Method in chapter five, where it was used to discuss the benefits of fostering critical thinking among employees. Here, we'll dive deeper into its uses in modern times.

Application in Modern Contexts

In today's world, where discussions can become echo chambers, the Socratic Method serves as a powerful antidote. It encourages you to engage deeply with different perspectives, creating a more nuanced understanding of the issues. For instance, in a business meeting, instead of simply nodding along to a proposed strategy, applying the Socratic Method would involve questioning the rationale behind the strategy, challenging its assumptions, and exploring its implications. This approach clarifies the thought processes behind decisions and exposes any flaws or weaknesses in the arguments, leading to more robust outcomes.

Questioning Foundations

Central to the Socratic Method is the practice of questioning the foundations of our beliefs and assumptions. This is not about doubting for doubting's sake but about ensuring that our convictions are built on solid ground. By regularly questioning the basis of your knowledge, you protect yourself against the risk of basing decisions on shaky assumptions or incomplete information. For example, if you believe that a project is guaranteed to succeed because similar projects have succeeded in the past, the Socratic Method would push you to examine whether those conditions still apply or if new variables are at play.

Practical Exercises

To integrate the Socratic Method into your daily life, start with scenarios that are familiar and non-threatening. Perhaps during a dinner conversation, pick an easy topic and practice asking more profound questions like:

- *"What makes you think that?"*
- *"How do you know this?"*
- *"Can you explain why this is important?"*

As you become more comfortable with the method, you can apply it to more complex issues. For instance, if you are considering a career change, question the underlying reasons for your dissatisfaction with your current job and what you truly seek in your professional life. You might be surprised at the answers you find when applying this method to your motivations and the clarity that it can provide.

Through these practices, the Socratic Method is a philosophical relic and a dynamic tool in modern critical thinking, applicable in personal introspections, workplace problem-solving, and civic engagement. By adopting this method, you engage in a more deliberate decision-making process, ensuring that your conclusions are well-founded and your actions aligned with your true intentions and values. The goal of this method is to encourage personal growth, foster a culture of more thoughtful dialogue, and make it easier to be informed in your decision-making when interacting with others.

8.2 COGNITIVE BEHAVIORAL TECHNIQUES FOR CRITICAL THINKERS

Understanding Cognitive Distortions

Imagine your brain as a photographer that sometimes gets the settings wrong. The pictures come out distorted: too dark, overly bright, or strangely angled. Cognitive distortions are similar—they are ways in which your mind convinces you of something false. These inaccurate thoughts usually reinforce negative thinking or emotions, telling you things like "You always fail," "You can't change this," or "Everything is terrible." Understanding these distortions is crucial because they can lead to harmful decisions and toxic patterns in both personal and professional realms. The first step towards mitigating these effects is to recognize common distortive patterns such as:

- **All-Or-Nothing Thinking:** Viewing situations in only two categories, perfect or disastrous.
- **Overgeneralization:** Drawing broad conclusions from a single event.
- **Catastrophizing:** Expecting the worst scenario to happen.

By identifying these patterns, you can start questioning them and gradually train your mind to adopt a more balanced and realistic perspective.

CBT Principles for Critical Thinking

Cognitive Behavioral Therapy (CBT) isn't just a therapeutic tool; it's also a powerhouse for enhancing critical thinking. At its core, CBT involves identifying negative and often irrational thoughts and systematically challenging them to align closer to reality. You can apply CBT principles to critical thinking by first noting when you're using cognitive distortions to process information. For instance, when faced with a challenging project, you might think, "I'm going to mess this up like everything else." That's your cue to apply CBT techniques:

- Evaluate this thought for accuracy.
- Challenge its validity.
- Replace it with a more constructive and realistic thought, such as, "I've faced similar challenges before and managed them with some effort."

This process helps you make more rational, less emotion-driven decisions and builds your confidence in handling complex situations.

Self-regulation and Emotional Control

The ability to regulate your emotions and remain calm under pressure is a hallmark of a great critical thinker. Emotional self-regulation in critical thinking means maintaining control over your emotional responses so that they don't cloud your judgment or decision-making processes. For example, if you receive feedback that's not particularly positive, instead of spiraling into self-doubt or defensiveness, use CBT techniques to manage your initial emotional response. Take a moment to breathe deeply and analyze the feedback logically to extract valuable insights. When you receive feedback, rather than viewing it as a personal attack, you can use critical thinking principles to guide you through seeing the value such feedback can provide. This ability to detach from immediate emotional responses and think things through logically prevents unnecessary stress and leads to more deliberate conclusions and actions.

Application to Personal and Professional Life

Integrating CBT techniques into your daily life can profoundly impact how you make decisions, solve problems, and interact with others. In personal contexts, this might look like reframing your thoughts to reduce anxiety about future uncertainties, allowing you to enjoy present moments more fully or make plans without undue stress. Professionally, CBT can transform how you handle workplace challenges. Consider a scenario where you're leading a team that's resistant to new changes you propose. Instead of concluding that the team is uncooperative, use CBT to assess why resistance exists, possibly identifying valid concerns you hadn't considered. Address these systematically by providing more information to alleviate uncertainties, thus facilitating a smoother transition. The key lies in continually practicing these techniques, making them a natural part of your thinking process and enhancing your overall effectiveness in navigating both personal and professional landscapes.

By leveraging the principles of CBT, you equip yourself with a robust toolkit for deconstructing and rebuilding your thought processes. This not only aids in diminishing the influence of cognitive distortions but also sharpens your ability to engage with the world in a more informed, balanced, and open-minded manner. Whether making a critical decision, solving a complex problem, or interacting with challenging personalities, these cognitive behavioral techniques ensure that your thinking remains clear, strategic, and, most importantly, effective. Through consistent practice, you'll find that your decisions are more sound and reached with a greater sense of confidence and peace.

8.3 THE ROLE OF INTUITION IN CRITICAL THINKING: WHEN TO TRUST YOUR GUT

Balancing Rationality and Intuition

In the vast decision-making landscape, the connection between rationality and intuition can sometimes resemble a dance—each step, whether based on hard data or a gut feeling, guides you to your next move. Understanding when to lean on rational analysis and when to trust your intuitive insights is crucial for making sound decisions. Rational thinking, relying on observable facts and logical inference, provides a solid foundation for critical thinking. It's like having a roadmap when navigating unfamiliar territory. However, intuition, which often draws from a deeper, less conscious pool of experiences and knowledge, can sometimes spot shortcuts and hidden paths not visible on the map. The key to balancing these two lies in recognizing each other's strengths and limitations. For instance, when time is of the essence, and data is scarce, intuition can provide a swift decision-making tool. Conversely, in high-stakes scenarios, where the consequences of decisions are significant, relying on a methodical, rational approach is advisable. By cultivating the ability to gauge when to utilize rationality and when to trust your intuition, you enhance your overall decision-making prowess, leading to outcomes that are effective and intuitively aligned with your goals and values.

Understanding the Gut Feeling

Delving into the nature of intuition, it's fascinating to consider its psychological and physiological roots. Psychologists suggest that intuition, often called a 'gut feeling,' is a rapid-fire, unconscious associative process that our brains revert to when making decisions. This process is influenced by our past experiences, emotions, and cognitive biases, which shape our instinctual reactions. From a physiological standpoint, intuition is also linked to our body's response systems. For instance, the 'gut feeling' you experience is partially due to the vagus nerve, which runs from the brain to the abdomen, playing a key role in transmitting signals of unease or comfort, thus influencing our decision-making process. Understanding this complex connection of mind and body can enhance the trust in your intuition, recognizing it as a sum of vast, often untapped knowledge about your environment and past experiences. This recognition simplifies intuition and elevates its role in complementing rational thought, mainly when logical data might be incomplete or unavailable.

Heuristics vs. Intuition

While both heuristics (previously discussed in Chapter 2) and intuition serve as tools for quick decision-making, distinguishing between the two is crucial for effective critical thinking. Heuristics are cognitive shortcuts that simplify decision-making by reducing the complex reality into more manageable units. They are like using rules of thumb based on patterns and generalizations. For example, a common heuristic is the 'availability heuristic,' where you might judge the probability of events based on how quickly and easily examples come to mind. Intuition, on the other hand, is more subtle and often arises from a deeper, sometimes unconscious, synthesis of experience and knowledge. It's not just a shortcut based on recognized patterns but a complex, instantaneous synthesis of accumulated wisdom. Understanding the difference helps decide when to rely on a quick heuristic rule and when to trust a deeper intuition. At its core, relying on a quick heuristic rule could be a pitfall to rational and critical thinking. By training your mind to think more critically, we can lean on our intuition more as our internal processes become more rational and constructive.

Developing Intuitive Intelligence

Enhancing your intuitive intelligence involves more than just trusting your gut; it requires active cultivation and refinement of this innate capability. One effective method to develop intuition is through mindfulness practices. Engaging in mindfulness meditation, for instance, can help you tune into your subconscious thoughts and feelings, which are the bedrock of intuition. These practices help quiet the noise of everyday life, allowing you to hear your inner voice more clearly. Another technique is to keep an intuition journal. Regularly record instances where you followed your intuition, noting the outcomes and the feelings associated with these decisions. Over time, this record will boost your confidence in your intuitive abilities and help you identify the situations where your intuition tends to be particularly strong or weak.

Additionally, exposing yourself to various experiences can enrich your intuitive database. The more diverse your experiences, the richer the reservoir of instincts you can draw upon when faced with new situations. By actively engaging in these practices, you not only refine your intuitive skills but also enhance your ability to integrate these insights with rational analysis, leading to a more holistic approach to problem-solving and decision-making.

8.4 DEVELOPING A CRITICAL THINKING MINDSET

Critical thinking isn't just a skill set; it's a mindset that involves distinct traits and attitudes that fundamentally change how you interact with the world. Like gardeners tending to crops, critical thinkers cultivate a rich landscape of ideas and possibilities, constantly tending to their intellectual soil to prevent it from becoming barren. The following key traits form the core of this mindset:

- Open-mindedness: Allows you to consider new ideas and alternatives, providing the flexibility to see beyond your initial perceptions.
- Skepticism: This is not about doubting everything for its own sake but involves questioning ideas and assertions to ensure they are well-supported, thus safeguarding against gullibility and errors in reasoning.
- Intellectual humility: Acknowledging the limits of your knowledge and encourages you to be receptive to learning from others, regardless of their status or position.

Cultivating curiosity is another cornerstone of the critical thinking mindset. It's the spark that ignites the desire to explore, ask questions, and seek understanding. Curiosity drives you to look beneath the surface, to unravel the threads of assumptions that weave through conventional wisdom. It pushes you to venture beyond the familiar confines of established knowledge, prompting you to challenge the status quo and explore new territories of thought. This relentless pursuit of knowledge isn't just about satisfying a personal quest; it's about enriching your understanding of and engagement with the world. You can nurture this trait by setting aside time for exploration and discovery, whether through reading, travel, or engaging in new experiences. Each new piece of knowledge you acquire feeds your curiosity, creating a self-sustaining cycle of learning and growth.

However, maintaining this mindset requires you to overcome intellectual complacency, which can settle in once you feel comfortable in your understanding of a subject. Intellectual complacency is akin to treading water; it might keep you afloat, but it won't move you forward. To combat this, you must continuously challenge your beliefs and remain open to new ideas and perspectives. This might involve playing devil's advocate with your own opinions, seeking out and considering the validity of opposing viewpoints, or simply admitting that you might be wrong in light of new evidence. Such practices prevent stagnation and deepen your critical engagement with issues, leading to a more robust and nuanced understanding.

Advocating for lifelong learning is essential to sustain and enhance your critical thinking skills. Lifelong learning is about embracing continuous education—not just in a formal academic sense but as a personal commitment to never stop learning. It's about recognizing that the world is a complex, ever-changing landscape of information where new discoveries are made daily, and the only way to keep up is to keep learning. This commitment can manifest in various forms, from taking up new hobbies that challenge your mental faculties, attending workshops and seminars relevant to your interests, or simply dedicating time each week to read about a new topic. Each learning experience adds layers to your understanding, equipping you with broader insights and more refined tools for critical analysis.

By actively developing these traits and practices, you transform thinking into an art form where each thought is carefully crafted, and each belief is rigorously tested. This mindset enhances your personal and professional life and contributes to a more informed, thoughtful, and discerning society.

8.5 THE POWER OF REFLECTIVE PRACTICE AND SELF-ASSESSMENT

Reflective practice is a transformative tool that turns everyday experiences into profound learning opportunities. It allows you to reflect on your actions, decisions, and experiences to gain insights to drive personal and professional growth. Think of it as having a rewind button, giving you the chance to review past scenarios with a critical eye, learn from them, and adjust future behaviors and strategies accordingly. This practice is particularly vital in a world where both personal and professional landscapes are rapidly evolving, demanding not just passive participation but active, reflective engagement to stay ahead. Whether you're reflecting on a project's outcome, a day's interactions, or a significant life decision, taking the time to step back and ponder the whys and hows can deepen your understanding and enhance your decision-making skills.

Techniques for Reflection

Several techniques can facilitate effective reflection, turning it into a structured and fruitful exercise. Journaling stands out for its simplicity and effectiveness. It involves regularly recording details of experiences and your reactions to them. This might be as straightforward as noting what went well in a meeting and what didn't and pondering how different approaches might have altered the outcome. Over time, this record becomes a valuable repository of personal insights and lessons learned. Another powerful technique is meditation, which allows for deeper, more focused reflection. It clears the mental clutter, facilitating a better connection with your inner thoughts and feelings. This can be particularly useful after intense experiences, providing the mental space needed to process events more deeply. Structured debriefing sessions can also be incredibly beneficial, whether solo or with a mentor or coach. These sessions should focus on dissecting events to understand what happened, why, and how similar situations could be handled better in the future. By incorporating these practices into your routine, you not only make reflection a regular part of your life but also enhance its quality and the insights it generates.

Self-Assessment Tools

Self-assessment tools can complement reflective practices and help you gauge your critical thinking skills and identify areas for improvement. These tools range from simple checklists and questionnaires designed to measure various aspects of critical thinking—such as logical reasoning, argument analysis, and decision-making—to more sophisticated tools like 360-degree feedback instruments that involve collecting perceptions about your thinking and behavior from colleagues and supervisors. These assessments provide concrete, often quantifiable, data that can highlight your strengths and pinpoint weaknesses in your thinking processes. Regularly engaging with these tools helps you track your progress over time and provides a clear direction for personal development efforts.

Action Planning

Armed with insights from reflective practice and concrete data from self-assessments, you're well-positioned to develop action plans that aim to fortify your critical thinking abilities. Effective action planning involves setting specific, achievable goals based on the insights gathered. For instance, if reflection and assessment reveal a tendency towards confirmation bias, you might set a goal to engage with a wider range of information sources or adopt practices like the devil's advocate approach to challenge your preconceptions. Each plan should include clear steps, resources needed, and timelines, making it actionable and measurable. Such targeted plans focus your efforts on areas that most need improvement and provide structured pathways to achieving your critical thinking goals.

By embedding reflective practices and self-assessment into your routine and strategically acting on the insights you gain, you transform passive experiences into active learning opportunities. This ongoing process sharpens your existing critical thinking skills. It prepares you to meet future challenges with greater agility and confidence. As you continue to engage with these practices, remember that each reflection, assessment, and action plan is a step towards not just better thinking but a more insightful, proactive approach to your personal and professional life.

As we wrap up this chapter, it's clear that the journey of enhancing your critical thinking skills is continuous and dynamic. From the ancient wisdom of the Socratic Method to modern cognitive behavioral techniques, each strategy discussed offers unique tools for refining your thinking. Next, we will explore how to extend these critical thinking strategies into broader community settings, enhancing individual decisions and contributing to collective wisdom and shared decision-making. This next chapter will bridge personal mastery with community influence, illustrating the ripple effect of strong critical thinking skills in larger pools of interaction.

Action Steps:

- **Practice the Socratic Method in Conversations:** During a casual conversation with a friend or colleague, pick a topic of discussion and use Socratic questioning to dig deeper into it. Aim to understand the underlying assumptions and logic behind the other person's viewpoints and gently challenge them to clarify and defend their positions.
- **Identify and Challenge Cognitive Distortions:** Familiarize yourself with the cognitive distortions discussed in this chapter. Pay attention to your thoughts throughout the day,

especially in response to stressful or challenging situations. When you notice a cognitive distortion, pause and ask yourself:
- *"Is this thought accurate?"*
- *"What evidence do I have for and against this thought?"*
- *"How can I reframe this thought to be more balanced and realistic?"*

CHAPTER 9
PROMOTING INSIGHTFUL THINKING IN COMMUNITIES

Critical thinking has uses beyond the internal atmosphere of your mind—it extends beyond you, your faculties, and your day. It can also enrich the lives of others and allow you to make a more significant positive impact in your community. In this chapter, we explore how to cultivate such enriching online and offline environments, weaving networks of thinkers who challenge, support, and inspire one another to reach new heights of insight and understanding.

BUILDING CRITICAL THINKING COMMUNITIES: ONLINE AND OFFLINE

Community Formation Principles

Creating a community focused on critical thinking requires ongoing care, perseverance, and a supportive atmosphere where all members can flourish. The first step to creating a community around critical thinking is establishing a foundation built on diversity and inclusivity. Diversity here isn't just about cultural or demographic differences but also about welcoming various perspectives, experiences, and areas of expertise. This variety enriches the community, as each member brings unique insights that can challenge group assumptions and broaden collective understanding. To ensure inclusivity, it's crucial to cultivate an atmosphere where every voice is valued—a place where members feel safe expressing dissenting views without fear of dismissal or ridicule. This can be encouraged by setting clear community guidelines that promote respectful interactions and actively moderating discussions to maintain a constructive and supportive tone.

Online Platforms

The digital age has revolutionized community formation, allowing us to connect with like-minded individuals worldwide. Online platforms are crucial in hosting virtual critical-thinking communities that transcend geographical boundaries. These platforms, such as forums, social media groups, and collaborative projects, foster diverse and dynamic exchanges of ideas, making critical thinking an accessible and daily practice. For instance, an online forum dedicated to critical thinking in science can connect a high school teacher in Brazil with a researcher in Norway, each contributing perspectives that enrich the other's understanding and approach. Building an engaged community by regularly introducing stimulating topics, recognizing active members, and encouraging a culture of mutual learning and respect is essential to fully harness these platforms' potential.

Offline Initiatives

While online platforms offer remarkable reach and convenience, offline communities provide the irreplaceable value of face-to-face interaction. Local book clubs, discussion groups, and educational collectives can transform theoretical knowledge of critical thinking into tangible, interpersonal experiences. For example, a local library might host a monthly critical thinking workshop where participants analyze current events through a critical lens, discussing and debating in real time. These gatherings strengthen community bonds and allow nuances and emotions to be conveyed more deeply, enhancing understanding and empathy among members. Another impactful initiative could be partnering with educational institutions to organize guest lectures and interactive sessions that foster critical thinking skills among students and the wider community.

Sustaining Engagement

Keeping a community engaged over time can be challenging but is crucial for its growth and sustainability. Regular events and challenges can keep the intellectual energy high.

Consider organizing monthly debates on controversial issues or collaborative projects that tackle real-world problems. These activities keep members intellectually stimulated and emotionally invested in the community. Moreover, celebrating milestones and achievements—such as the publication of a member's research paper or the successful organization of a community-led conference—can boost morale and reinforce a sense of collective purpose. For instance, you can host a special event to acknowledge these achievements or create a section on your platform highlighting these milestones. Another effective strategy is to rotate leadership roles within the community, giving members a sense of ownership and responsibility that can drive sustained involvement and commitment.

By weaving together these threads of diversity, digital connectivity, face-to-face interaction, and continuous engagement, you can create a tapestry of critical-thinking communities that are as vibrant and dynamic as they are insightful and impactful. Whether online or offline, these communities hold the power to transform individual perspectives and foster a culture of deep, critical engagement with the world. In the following sections, we will explore how these principles apply specifically in educational settings, through workshops and events, and by leveraging technology to further enhance and expand the reach of critical thinking initiatives.

9.2 CRITICAL THINKING IN EDUCATION: STRATEGIES FOR TEACHERS

Curriculum Integration

Integrating critical thinking into the educational curriculum isn't just about adding a new subject; it's about weaving it into the fabric of existing subjects, from humanities to STEM. This process involves rethinking how and what we teach, ensuring that critical thinking becomes integral to learning at every stage. In the humanities, this could mean encouraging students to learn historical facts and analyze the causes and implications of historical events. How did certain decisions lead to specific outcomes? What were the possible alternatives? This analytical approach can be mirrored in literature classes by examining characters' motivations and the consequences of their actions rather than merely recounting plots.

Integrating critical thinking in STEM requires shifting from memory-based to inquiry-based learning. Instead of only teaching students to solve equations, teachers could present real-world problems that require students to apply mathematical concepts to develop solutions. Science classes could focus on experimental design, encouraging students to hypothesize, experiment, and critically analyze their results. What did the experiment show, and just as importantly, what didn't it show? By embedding these questions into lessons, educators foster a mindset that values thoughtful exploration over mere memorization.

Active Learning Techniques

Active learning techniques are pivotal in transforming passive classrooms into dynamic environments where critical thinking thrives; techniques like problem-based learning place students in the driver's seat, giving them real-world problems without predefined solutions. Here, the role of the teacher shifts from imparting knowledge to facilitating a learning experience where students engage deeply with content, collaborate with peers, and navigate the complexities of problem-solving. For instance, in a problem-based learning scenario, students might be tasked with designing a sustainable energy solution for their school. This task requires them to research, apply scientific principles, and weigh ethical considerations, thereby honing their critical thinking skills in a meaningful context.

Debates and case studies are also effective in promoting critical thinking. Debates force students to understand multiple sides of an issue, develop persuasive arguments, and critically evaluate the opposing viewpoints. In a social studies class, a discussion on the merits of a policy can help students understand its complexity and potential impacts on different groups of people. On the other hand, case studies provide a rich context for students to apply theoretical knowledge in practical scenarios, whether analyzing a business case in an economics class or diagnosing a patient in a health sciences course. These activities keep students engaged and develop essential analytical thinking and decision-making skills.

Assessment of Critical Thinking

Assessing critical thinking in educational settings can be challenging, as it goes beyond right or wrong answers. It requires a focus on how students arrive at those answers—their reasoning, the breadth of evidence they consider, and their ability to connect disparate pieces of information. Formative assessments, which provide ongoing feedback during the learning process, are particularly effective in nurturing critical thinking skills. These can include reflective journals, where students articulate their thought processes and learning experiences, or concept maps that require them to illustrate connections between ideas. Such assessments help teachers identify students' understanding and misconceptions in real-time, allowing for timely interventions that guide students toward deeper analytical thinking.

Reflective practices should also be integrated into the assessment process. Encouraging students to reflect on their learning and thought processes can deepen their understanding and enhance their critical thinking skills. This could be facilitated through end-of-unit reflections where students discuss what strategies helped them understand complex concepts and where they struggled. This not only aids in self-assessment but also helps educators tailor future lessons to better meet students' needs.

Teacher Training and Development

Teachers must be adept at critical thinking to be effectively integrated into education. This underscores the importance of professional development in critical-thinking apprentices. Ongoing training programs can equip teachers with the latest tools and techniques in critical thinking instruction, from structuring discussions that provoke thoughtful analysis to creating assignments that challenge students to delve deeper into the material. Workshops or professional learning communities can provide platforms for teachers to practice these skills and share best practices. Additionally, schools can foster a culture of critical thinking among staff by encouraging interdisciplinary teaching approaches that allow teachers to blend different subjects, thereby modeling critical thinking through curriculum integration.

By investing in teacher training, schools ensure that educators are not just conveyors of knowledge but facilitators of deep, meaningful learning. This investment pays dividends across the educational spectrum, as teachers play a crucial role in shaping the next generation of thinkers and leaders. As educators, embracing these strategies transforms your teaching practice and profoundly impacts your students' ability to navigate the complex world with discernment and insight.

9.3 ORGANIZING CRITICAL THINKING WORKSHOPS AND EVENTS

When you think about organizing a workshop or an event that will promote critical thinking or better your community, there are probably a lot of thoughts and options that spring into your mind. Tackling these problems one step at a time will be crucial for designing a workshop that engages and challenges the participants in your community. It should involve a blend of structured activities and open-ended discussions that will encourage a deeper exploration of ideas, even after they leave the event. Start by defining the goals of the workshop. Are you aiming to enhance problem-solving skills or foster better decision-making? These goals will guide the structure of your sessions. For example, the focus is on developing argumentative skills. In that case, you might structure the workshop around a debate, providing participants with pre-selected topics and resources to help them build their cases. To stimulate engagement, incorporate interactive elements like real-time polls or group problem-solving scenarios that relate directly to the participants' daily lives or professional challenges. This practical application helps bridge the theoretical aspects of critical thinking with tangible, real-world actions.

Moving on to the logistics of planning and promoting such events, the key lies in understanding your audience and tailoring the experience to meet their needs. Identifying the target audience helps select the most suitable venue, timing, and promotional strategies. For instance, if your target audience is busy professionals, consider hosting the event in a central business district or offering an option for virtual participation. Promotion strategies should leverage channels your audience frequents; for professionals, this might mean LinkedIn ads or partnerships with industry associations. Early bird registration discounts or providing certificates of participation can also boost early interest and registrations.

Remember, the clarity of communication in your promotional materials—clearly stating the benefits, learning outcomes, and any prerequisites—will help potential participants understand the value of the event and how it aligns with their personal or professional growth objectives.

Effective facilitation is crucial for the success of any workshop, especially one dealing with something as dynamic and potentially divisive as critical thinking. Facilitators must be adept at presenting information, managing diverse viewpoints, and steering discussions constructively. Techniques like the 'think-pair-share' can be instrumental; participants first think through a problem independently, then discuss their thoughts with a partner, and finally share their conclusions with the larger group. This technique encourages quieter participants to engage and helps prevent dominant personalities from overtaking the conversation. Another helpful approach is using case studies or hypothetical scenarios that require participants to apply their critical thinking skills to develop solutions. These should be carefully chosen to be relevant and challenging enough to stimulate discussion but not so complex that they become frustrating.

Finally, the importance of follow-up activities and community building must be considered. The end of the workshop should not be the end of the learning journey. Follow-up activities include online forums where participants can continue discussions or scheduled reunion webinars to revisit the topics, help maintain the momentum, and deepen the learning experience. Additionally, encouraging participants to form smaller, peer-led groups can help them to keep practicing and refining their critical thinking skills in a supportive environment. Sharing additional resources, like articles, books, or videos that delve deeper into the workshop topics, can also enhance ongoing learning and engagement. By fostering a community of practice, you extend the workshop's impact and build a network of individuals committed to personal and collective growth through critical thinking. These communities can become self-sustaining, with members eventually stepping up to lead discussions or mentor new participants, thereby ensuring the longevity and continued relevance of the community.

9.4 LEVERAGING TECHNOLOGY TO PROMOTE COLLECTIVE CRITICAL THINKING

In the digital age, our tools can significantly amplify our capabilities. When it comes to fostering critical thinking, technology offers some unique advantages. Digital tools and platforms have the power to break down geographical barriers, enabling collective intelligence to flourish across borders. A great example is shared document platforms like Google Docs or Microsoft OneDrive. These tools allow multiple users to work on the same document in real time, making collaboration seamless. Imagine a scenario where team members worldwide analyze data, brainstorm ideas, and refine strategies on a single document. The immediacy and transparency of these platforms speed up the process and enhance the richness of inputs as diverse perspectives converge to challenge and refine each other's thoughts.

Having mind-mapping tools can offer another dimension of collaborative critical thinking. These tools allow users to visually represent their thoughts and ideas, linking concepts and identifying relationships in a dynamic, intuitive layout. Mind maps can be particularly useful in complex projects involving multiple stakeholders, as they help clarify the structure of thoughts and ideas, making the connections between them explicit. This visual arrangement often leads to new insights as it encourages a holistic view of the problem or topic at hand. Moreover, these tools frequently support collaborative functionalities, allowing team members to contribute simultaneously, each adding their layer of analysis, questioning, and refinement.

Discussion forums, especially those dedicated to specific topics or industries, can also be powerful platforms for collective critical thinking. Platforms like Stack Exchange or specialized LinkedIn groups offer spaces where questions can be posed, ideas debated, and solutions proposed within a community of professionals and enthusiasts. The strength of these forums lies in the cumulative knowledge of their members, who bring a broad range of experiences and expertise to the table. Here, critical thinking is sharpened against the whetstone of public scrutiny and peer review, often leading to robust and innovative solutions.

Moving into online learning communities, these are designed around the core idea of continuous, collaborative learning. Platforms like this provide courses and foster communities where learners can discuss course materials, pose questions, and share insights. These interactions enrich the learning experience, embedding it within a social context miming real-life problem-solving scenarios. Managing such communities effectively involves a balance of professional moderation and peer-to-peer interaction, ensuring that discussions remain focused and productive. The community managers often play a pivotal role in guiding conversations, highlighting insightful contributions, and bringing in expert opinions when necessary.

The concept of gamification has proven to be a game-changer in engaging users in online learning. By integrating elements typical of game playing (e.g.), point scoring, competition with others, rules of play) Gamification can help develop critical thinking skills that are more engaging and enjoyable in learning activities. For instance, a digital learning platform might incorporate badges and leaderboards as part of a course on logical reasoning, where learners earn points for each level of complexity they master in problem-solving. Such elements can motivate learners to delve deeper and apply their skills more rigorously, all within a framework that feels more like play than work.

When it comes to evaluating the effectiveness of these digital resources and technologies, several criteria stand out. The first is user engagement—tools that are intuitive and enjoyable to use are likely to sustain users' interest over time. Next is the depth of interaction the tool supports; platforms that allow for rich interaction, whether through multimedia content, real-time collaboration, or community discussion, tend to facilitate more meaningful learning and insight. Another crucial factor is accessibility; tools that are easily accessible, not just in terms of cost but also in terms of usability, ensure that a wider audience can benefit from them.

Lastly, measuring a tool's impact on actual learning outcomes is critical. This can be assessed through direct feedback from users and through more formal evaluation methods such as pre-and post-tests or case studies demonstrating how the tool has been used to solve actual problems.

As we wrap up this exploration of how technology can enhance collective critical thinking, it's clear that the digital tools at our disposal are more than just conveniences; they are catalysts for creating more prosperous, more inclusive, and dynamic intellectual ecosystems. By leveraging these tools, we expand the scope and scale of our collaborative efforts and deepen the impact of our collective intelligence. As we move into the next chapter, we will explore how the future of critical thinking is being shaped by these technological advancements, setting the stage for a world where collective wisdom drives progress and innovation.

Action Steps:

- **Join and Participate:** Engage in online forums and offline discussion groups dedicated to critical thinking. Contribute diverse perspectives and respect others' viewpoints to foster a supportive community atmosphere.
- **Attend and Organize Events:** Attend workshops, debates, and local educational initiatives focused on critical thinking. Organize or participate in events that promote interactive learning and deepen understanding through face-to-face interactions.

- **Utilize Digital Tools:** Explore digital platforms for collaboration, such as shared documents and online forums. Join online learning communities to continue discussions, share insights, and enhance critical thinking skills beyond traditional educational settings.

CHAPTER 10
THE FUTURE OF CRITICAL THINKING

Our world is more connected now than ever before; we can see the effects of one decision ripple across continents within an hour. In such a world, critical thinking is not just a personal asset but a global imperative. It's the compass that guides us through complex terrains of cultural differences, political conflicts, and international crises. This chapter explores how critical thinking shapes our global community, builds cross-cultural cooperation, drives educational reforms, and helps prepare leaders for the ever-changing world.

10.1 THE GLOBAL IMPLICATIONS OF CRITICAL THINKING

Critical Thinking in a Global Context

When information travels at the speed of light, the butterfly effect is real and palpable—actions taken in one part of the world can have significant consequences elsewhere. Consider climate change, a critical issue that knows no borders. It demands a global response, yet this response is mired in diverse political, economic, and cultural perspectives that often lead to conflict rather than cooperation. Here, critical thinking becomes vital in understanding the science and navigating the socio-political landscapes that determine our response to it. For instance, when negotiating international agreements, diplomats must critically evaluate the environmental impact, economic implications, and national interests that play into decision-making processes. In situations like these, we can see the effect of using principles of critical thinking. It can not only make your life easier, but when those same ideas are replicated by world leaders, the effects can be considerable.

Moreover, public health crises such as pandemics and viral outbreaks underscore the importance of critical thinking at all levels. When misinformation spreads as quickly as a virus, critically assessing information becomes crucial. The global spread of a virus highlights the need for critical evaluation of the vast amounts of shared data and recommendations, with individuals needing to discern between expert advice and misleading information. On a governmental level, critical thinking is vital in balancing public health measures with economic impacts, a decision-making process that influences global markets and travel policies.

Cross-Cultural Perspectives

As our world becomes increasingly multicultural, the ability to navigate and respect cultural differences is paramount. Critical thinking offers a lens through which we can understand and appreciate the complexity of various cultural norms and practices without judgment. This is not about finding a "one size fits all" approach but about recognizing and respecting diversity. In multinational companies, for example, leaders must make decisions that are aware of cultural sensitivities and practices. A critical thinker in this context would consider the cultural nuances that influence employee interactions, communication styles, and leadership perceptions. They would tailor management strategies to fit diverse workplace environments and find ones that enhance cooperation and productivity. They would understand the benefit of growing an inclusive corporate culture that values diversity and leverages the broad range of expertise they've cultivated.

Global Education Initiatives

Education systems worldwide increasingly recognize the importance of instilling critical thinking skills from an early age. Some international educational programs have made critical thinking a core component of their curriculum, emphasizing its significance across subjects. These programs prepare students for academic success and global citizenship, equipping them to question, analyze, and engage with the world around them thoughtfully and respectfully. We are more consistently seeing global education initiatives involve exchange programs. These collaborations help expose students to different ways of thinking and problem-solving, not just growing their understanding of the world but also how they can apply critical thinking practices at home and abroad.

Future Global Leaders

The leaders of tomorrow face a world that is more complex and interconnected than ever before. To navigate this world, they must be adept at critical thinking and applying this skill in varied, often volatile environments. Future leaders must be prepared to deal with complex global systems, understanding how changes in one part of the system can impact others. They'll need to think critically about global economics, environmental sustainability, and technological advancements, often all at once. Training for such leadership starts with education but continues through lifelong learning and practice. Earlier, we mentioned the butterfly effect, the idea that the flap of a butterfly's wings can cause a hurricane in another part of the world. When we look at the ripple effects of implementing critical thinking, we can see how we can increase the personal and collective good. The sustained education of critical thinking concepts and training on using them in daily life can have a wide-ranging impact.

As we look to the future, the role of critical thinking in a global context becomes increasingly evident. It's about more than just solving problems—it's about understanding the origin of the issue itself. It goes beyond solving the problem but asks the additional questions of 'Why?' and 'How?' This global perspective on critical thinking enriches individual minds and enhances collective efforts to tackle some of the most pressing challenges of our time. As we navigate this complex global landscape, cultivating critical thinking skills across cultures and continents remains crucial for creating a more thoughtful, informed, and cooperative world.

10.2 THE ROLE OF CRITICAL THINKING IN DEMOCRACY AND CIVIC ENGAGEMENT

Informed Citizenship

Democracy. A powerful word with a wide range of emotions attached to it. You may have a reactive response to reading the word. At its core understanding, democracy believes in utilizing the individual to implement change. A reliance on one's ability to think critically hinges on a citizen's ability to thoughtfully engage with the issues. Critical thinking empowers you, as a citizen, to sift through political rhetoric and media spin, allowing you to grasp the underlying issues at stake. It encourages you to question policies and proposals: What are their implications? Who benefits? Who might be disadvantaged? By engaging in this level of analysis, you become not just a voter but an informed participant in your democracy. This is crucial because democracies thrive on their citizens' active and informed involvement. Critical thinking leads to more considered and rational choices, promoting a political culture that values evidence over manipulation and sound arguments over sensational claims. When you hear news stories, read policies, or investigate regulations and practices, it's important to remember these ideals. It is always the right time to ask questions and use critical thinking to make consistently informed decisions.

Media Literacy

In the age of information overload, the ability to critically evaluate the torrent of news and information that regularly bombards us becomes more important each day. Media literacy, a crucial aspect of critical thinking, involves understanding how media messages are crafted and what agendas they may serve, even from sources that share your beliefs. It enables you to distinguish between credible news and misleading propaganda. Media literacy helps you understand different media outlets' biases and how these biases can shape the news. For example, recognizing that a news outlet consistently presents issues from a particular political viewpoint can prompt you to seek additional sources to get a more balanced view. Moreover, media literacy fosters a deeper understanding of the media's role in shaping public opinion and the implications this has for democracy. By critically engaging with media, you contribute to a public discourse that values truth and resists manipulation, strengthening the foundations of a democratic society and not just surrendering to the loudest point of view.

Public Discourse

Public discourse is the lifeblood of democracy, and its quality is directly influenced by the critical thinking skills of those who participate in it. Practical public discourse involves more than just exchanging opinions; it's about arguing constructively, recognizing valid points even in arguments you disagree with, and revising your views when presented with compelling evidence. Critical thinking elevates public discourse by encouraging such practices. It enables you to engage in debates constructively rather than in a divisive way. This is particularly important in a democratic society where differing views are inevitable, and the ability to negotiate and find common ground is essential for social cohesion and collective decision-making. For instance, a community debate over local school funding can benefit immensely from participants who, equipped with critical thinking skills, can evaluate data on educational outcomes, assess the merits of funding proposals, and engage in reasoned discussions that lead to equitable and practical solutions.

Civic Education

To nurture a generation of informed citizens capable of sustaining a healthy democracy, critical thinking must be an integral part of civic education. Schools play a pivotal role in this by teaching students about the structure and functions of government and empowering them with the skills to question, analyze, and evaluate. Civic education that incorporates critical thinking helps students understand the practical implications of civic issues and the importance of their participation in democracy. It prepares them to be not just passive recipients of civic knowledge but active, engaged citizens who can influence democratic processes and hold leaders accountable. For example, a civic education program that challenges students to design a campaign on a local issue teaches them about the political process practically while also honing their ability to think critically about strategies, messaging, and the ethical dimensions of political engagement.

Through these lenses, the role of critical thinking in democracy and civic engagement becomes clear. It's about empowering you with the knowledge, skills, and disposition necessary to engage fully and thoughtfully in the civic life of your community and country. As we face complex social, economic, and environmental challenges, the need for critically engaged citizens has never been greater. Whether it's through informed voting, media literacy, constructive public discourse, or comprehensive civic education, critical thinking is vital to nurturing a democratic society that is not only resilient but also capable of evolving and adapting in response to new challenges.

10.3 ARTIFICIAL INTELLIGENCE AND CRITICAL THINKING: COEXISTING WITH SMART TECHNOLOGIES

Artificial Intelligence (AI) is no longer just a buzzword in sci-fi movies but a significant part of our daily interactions. Even as this process develops, it's essential to understand how this technology intersects with how the human brain works, especially with critical thinking. AI systems, from simple algorithms that filter your email to complex machines capable of diagnosing diseases, are becoming integral to decision-making in various sectors. While the infusion of AI into these processes offers remarkable efficiency and opens new avenues for innovation, it also raises a critical question: does AI augment human critical thinking, or does it risk undermining it by encouraging complacency?

The relationship between AI and human decision-making is nuanced. On one hand, AI can significantly enhance our decision-making capabilities by processing and analyzing vast amounts of data faster than any human could. For instance, this capability can substantially benefit healthcare, where AI algorithms help diagnose diseases from imaging scans with accuracy rates that rival or surpass human experts. Here, AI acts not just as a tool but as a partner in the decision-making process, providing insights derived from patterns in data that might be too subtle for human eyes. However, this reliance on AI also raises concerns about human decision-makers becoming too dependent on automated systems, potentially weakening their critical thinking skills. When decisions are outsourced to algorithms, there is a risk that individuals will accept AI-generated conclusions without sufficient examination. Maintaining a balance where AI supports rather than supplants human judgment becomes imperative, ensuring that critical thinking remains at the forefront of decision-making processes.

Ethical considerations in AI development and deployment are broad and complex, touching on issues from privacy and security to fairness and transparency. Developing AI systems often involves using large datasets, including sensitive personal information. Here, critical thinking plays a role in the technical aspects of using this data and in considering the ethics of how this data is collected and shared. Moreover, as AI systems increasingly make decisions affecting people's lives, from job screening to loan approvals, the potential for biases—introduced through biased data sets or algorithmic design—becomes a significant ethical concern. What this means, in short, is that if AI learns incorrect or biased information, it can repeat that mistake over and over again, affecting many people's lives in the process. Critical thinkers must scrutinize AI systems for potential biases and ensure that these systems operate fairly and transparently. For example, when an AI system is used for hiring, it is crucial to examine not just the efficiency of the system but also whether it inadvertently discriminates against certain groups of applicants. This examination requires a deep understanding of both the technology and the socio-cultural contexts in which it operates.

Collaboration between humans and AI systems can yield extraordinary results, provided there is a cooperative relationship where each party's strengths are leveraged. Consider the field of disaster response, where AI can analyze satellite imagery to quickly identify areas hardest hit by a natural disaster. At the same time, human teams can make nuanced decisions about where and how to deploy limited resources most effectively. In such collaborations, critical thinking enhances the interaction by enabling humans to interpret and use AI-generated data in contextually appropriate ways. It involves questioning the limitations of AI recommendations, understanding the broader implications, and making decisions considering the ethical, social, and long-term consequences beyond the potential short-term gains of those actions.

Preparing for an AI-integrated future involves more than just technological readiness; it requires a commitment to developing robust critical thinking skills that can adapt to and work alongside evolving AI technologies. As AI becomes more sophisticated and embedded in all aspects of life, the ability to critically assess these technologies—understanding their workings, implications, and limitations—becomes crucial. Strategies for maintaining and enhancing critical thinking in an AI-driven world include:

- Integrating AI topics in education curricula.
- Promoting interdisciplinary learning that combines technology education with humanities and social sciences.
- Fostering continuous professional development that keeps pace with technological advancements.

For instance, a professional workshop on AI in the workplace could provide technical training and ethical case studies that encourage participants to think critically about how they deploy AI tools.

In navigating the complexities introduced by AI, the synergy between human critical thinking and machine intelligence offers a path forward that maximizes the benefits of technology while minimizing its risks. In every instance, our use of AI technologies should aid, not hinder, cooperation instead of becoming complacent. We cannot rely on AI to implement the critical thinking practices we learn. Still, we can harness the potential of machine learning to assist us responsibly.

10.4 LIFELONG LEARNING: KEEPING YOUR CRITICAL THINKING SKILLS SHARP

Lifelong learning can be scary and intimidating, but being a forever student is crucial for progress. The more the world changes, the more we must keep up and evolve our understanding with sound critical thinking practices. Continuous learning isn't merely about acquiring new information but refining and expanding your ability to think critically in various contexts, ensuring your skills remain sharp and applicable.

Let's take a moment to consider the following: The skills you learned a decade ago may no longer be sufficient for tackling today's challenges. As societal norms and technologies evolve, so too must our approaches to problem-solving and decision-making. This is where lifelong learning comes into play. It ensures that your critical thinking skills do not stagnate but evolve, keeping you capable of facing modern challenges. Engaging regularly in activities that challenge your intellect and force you to think in new ways is crucial. This could be as simple as reading books that push the boundaries of your understanding or as involved as taking part in workshops and seminars that explore novel concepts and perspectives.

The resources available for continuous learning in critical thinking are vast and varied, catering to every learning style and schedule. Online courses, for instance, offer flexibility and a breadth of subjects that can be tailored to your specific interests or needs. There are online platforms that host courses from universities worldwide on topics ranging from philosophy to business strategy, many of which are designed to enhance your critical thinking. Workshops, whether online or in person, can provide more interactive opportunities for honing your skills. These are often more focused on practical applications and offer the added benefit of learning from and with others, which can introduce new viewpoints and approaches to your repertoire. Additionally, the traditional reading route remains one of the most accessible and effective ways to support lifelong learning. Books, articles, and journals can expose you to advanced concepts and different cultural perspectives, deepening your critical thinking capabilities.

Creating a personal learning plan can dramatically increase the effectiveness of your lifelong learning efforts. This plan acts as a roadmap, outlining areas where you want to develop your critical thinking skills and setting clear, achievable objectives. Start by assessing your current critical thinking abilities. Identify strengths to build on and weaknesses that need improvement. This could involve self-assessment tools or feedback from colleagues and mentors. Based on this assessment, set specific goals. Perhaps you want to improve your ability to analyze data, understand logical fallacies more deeply, or become better at argumentation. Identify resources and activities for each goal that will help you achieve them. This might mean enrolling in a statistics course, participating in debate clubs, or scheduling regular study sessions on logical theory. Importantly, your learning plan should be dynamic, adapting as your skills improve and as your personal and professional needs change.

Adapting your critical thinking skills to keep pace with changes in society and technology is not just beneficial; it's essential. As new technologies emerge and societal issues shift, the context in which you apply your critical thinking skills transforms. For instance, the rise of social media has changed how we interact with information and each other, creating new challenges for critical thinking, such as the need to quickly identify credible sources and understand complex, often polarized, public issues. Similarly, advancements in technology like AI and machine learning are changing the workplace, demanding new kinds of analytical skills and ethical considerations. Staying informed about these changes and understanding how they impact your environment allows you to effectively adapt your critical thinking approaches. This might mean learning new methodologies for information assessment or exploring ethical frameworks for interacting with AI-driven systems.

In essence, lifelong learning is about maintaining the agility of your mind, enabling you to continue to apply critical thinking effectively as contexts change and new challenges arise. It supports personal growth and professional adaptability, ensuring you remain a valuable team member and a thoughtful community participant no matter what the future holds. Committing to continuous learning and regularly updating your skills ensures that your critical thinking remains a sharp tool in your intellectual arsenal, ready to tackle whatever challenges and opportunities life presents.

10.5 CREATING A PERSONAL CRITICAL THINKING PLAN: NEXT STEPS AND RESOURCES

Embarking on the road to bolstering your critical thinking skills involves more than just understanding the concepts; it requires a structured approach that includes assessing where you currently stand, setting clear and attainable goals, identifying the resources that can guide and support you, and committing to consistent practice. The approach should be tailored to you and your journey in a way that builds on your understanding of critical thinking. Use the information you've learned here to minimize mistakes and motivate you to pursue personal and professional objectives.

Assessing Your Critical Thinking Skills

The first step in any growth plan is understanding your starting point. Assessing your current critical thinking skills can sometimes feel like trying to look at a reflection in moving water—challenging but not impossible. Start by reflecting on recent situations where you needed to solve a problem or make a decision. Ask yourself: How did I approach it? Did I consider multiple perspectives? How well did I evaluate the evidence? You can use the action steps in previous chapters, notes, and journals you've kept to help with this process. These essential steps allow you to analyze why you thought a particular way about something and recognize patterns. Additionally, seeking feedback from trusted colleagues or mentors can offer an external perspective on your critical thinking abilities. They might point out biases you weren't aware of or commend the thoroughness of your analysis, which can help pinpoint areas of strength and those needing improvement.

Setting Personal Goals

Once you have a clear understanding of your critical thinking skills, the next step is setting goals that are not just aspirational but also achievable. Employing the SMART criteria—**S**pecific, **M**easurable, **A**chievable, **R**elevant, and **T**ime-bound—can structure this process effectively. For example, if you've identified a need to improve your ability to identify logical fallacies, a SMART goal could be: "By the end of the quarter, I will be able to identify and correctly name at least five different logical fallacies in the discussions during our team meetings." This goal is specific (identifying fallacies), measurable (at least five), achievable (with study and practice), relevant (valuable in meetings), and time-bound (by the end of the quarter). Setting well-defined goals ensures that your efforts are focused and your progress is trackable, significantly increasing the likelihood of success.

Identifying Resources and Support

No journey is undertaken alone, and the path to growing your critical thinking skills is no exception. Identifying the right resources and support mechanisms can make the process smoother and more enjoyable. Numerous resources are available, from books and articles that deepen your understanding of critical thinking concepts to online courses that offer structured learning experiences. Online platforms often provide courses designed to enhance critical thinking skills, often with interactive elements like peer discussions and practical exercises that enrich your learning experience.

Additionally, joining communities, whether online forums, local meetups, or professional networks, can provide ongoing support and motivation. These communities offer opportunities to engage with like-minded individuals, share challenges and solutions, and receive encouragement and feedback that can significantly improve your learning journey.

Commitment to Practice

Lastly, developing your critical thinking lies in regular practice and reflection. Just as a musician plays scales daily or an athlete runs drills, a critical thinker must continuously engage in activities that challenge and refine their thinking. This could be as simple as dedicating a few minutes each day to analyze a complex news article or as involved as participating in monthly debate clubs. The key is consistency. Additionally, setting aside time for regular reflection on what you've learned and how you've applied it helps cement these skills. Reflective practices reinforce learning and highlight areas requiring more focus or a different approach, allowing you to adjust your learning plan as needed.

In wrapping up this exploration into creating a personal critical thinking plan, remember that the goal is to build a scaffold that supports your continuous growth and adaptation as a thinker. By assessing your skills, setting targeted goals, leveraging diverse resources, and committing to regular practice, you equip yourself with the tools to improve your critical thinking skills and integrate them deeply into your personal and professional life.

CONGRATULATIONS!

You've reached the end of the book, but not the end of your critical thinking journey.

Completing this book signifies more than just turning the last page—it represents a significant investment in your intellectual growth. By engaging with the concepts and exercises, you've not only deepened your understanding of critical thinking but also equipped yourself with valuable tools that will enhance your decision-making and problem-solving abilities now and in the future.

As you move forward with the new skills and insights you've gained, we would love to hear about your experience and how the book has impacted you.

Scan the QR code below to visit our review page!

Once again, congratulations on your accomplishment! We're excited for you to put your newfound knowledge into practice and see the positive impact it will have on your life.

Thank you for being part of this journey and for your invaluable feedback.

Warmest regards,

Over The Horizon Team

CONCLUSION

As we conclude our transformative journey through the intricate pathways of critical thinking, I want to reflect on the ground we've covered. It's been a journey of profound change, from the foundational skills outlined in the early chapters to the more nuanced applications in your professional, personal, and digital interactions. We've progressed from understanding the basics to applying these critical skills across various parts of your daily life.

What we've covered in this book highlights a crucial aspect: critical thinking is now more than just a skill. It's become necessary for navigating our world and balancing our lives. With the barrage of information that hits us daily, the ability to sift through noise, analyze facts, and reach well-reasoned conclusions is indispensable. The ability to critically think about problems, manage your expectations, and balance your responsibilities keeps your life and relationships from tripping over each other for your attention. Building confidence with critical thinking has a ripple effect that doesn't just affect you here, at this moment, but touches different aspects of your life in broadening ways.

One key takeaway from our time together is the versatility of critical thinking. Whether you're evaluating a news article, making a strategic decision at work, or navigating the challenges of digital communication, the principles of critical thinking apply. It's this adaptability that makes your new skills not just helpful but essential.

Often, when people talk about developing skills, they'll tout them as 'life-changing' or 'profound.' The critical thing to recognize here is that while reading this book, developing these habits can be transformative; these skills and talents are something anyone can develop. Humans naturally can think critically; you need to practice and hone that craft, which allows you to turn obstacles into opportunities for growth and learning.

I urge you not to let this be the end of your critical thinking journey. Commit to challenging yourself with new puzzles and problems. Seek out interactions that expose you to different perspectives and keep your mind open and curious. The landscape of knowledge is vast and ever-changing, and maintaining your critical thinking skills requires continuous practice and engagement.

I also encourage you to become an advocate for critical thinking. Share these skills with your family, introduce them in your workplace, and discuss them in your community. The ripple effect of spreading critical thinking can bring about significant changes, not just in individual lives but across societies. I urge you to share what you've learned and inspire others to embark on their own critical thinking journey.

In summary, I want to thank you for going on this journey with me. The lessons in this book were designed to be simple and easy to implement in your daily life. Some of the concepts, such as discussing critical thinking and world leaders, were done to highlight the importance of developing these skills and their far-reaching implications. At the end of the day, no matter who you are or where you are in life, you can use these critical thinking practices to ask questions and uncover solutions.

Thank you for your time, and attention. This isn't the end of your journey; it's just the beginning.

REFERENCES

History of logic | Ancient, Medieval, Modern, & ... https://www.britannica.com/topic/history-of logic

Cognitive bias: What it is and how to overcome it - BetterUp https://www.betterup.com/blog/cognitive-bias

How can reasoning skills make you a better decision maker? https://www.linkedin.com/advice/3/how-can-reasoning-skills-make-you-better-decision

Mind Maps® - A Powerful Approach to Note-Taking - Mind Tools https://www.mindtools.com/ahlezc4/mind-maps

15 Logical Fallacies to Know, With Definitions and Examples https://www.grammarly.com/blog/logical-fallacies/

Advantages and Disadvantages of Open-Ended and Close ... https://monkeylearn.com/blog/advantages-of-open-ended-questions

Heuristics: Definition, Examples, and How They Work https://www.verywellmind.com/what-is-a-heuristic-2795235

Evaluating Internet Resources https://library.georgetown.edu/tutorials/research-guides/evaluating-internet-content

Echo chamber effects on short video platforms - PMC - NCBI https://www.ncbi.nlm.nih.gov/pmc/articles/PMC10111082/

Tackling Misinformation: A Three-Pronged Approach https://www.nih.gov/about-nih/what-we-do/science-health-public-trust/perspectives/tackling-misinformation-three-pronged-approach

The Digital Literacy Imperative https://www.csis.org/analysis/digital-literacy-imperative

A Leader's Framework for Decision Making https://hbr.org/2007/11/a-leaders-framework-for-decision-making

Financial Literacy: What It Is, and Why It Is So Important to ... https://www.investopedia.com/terms/f/financial-literacy.asp

Improving Emotional Intelligence (EQ) https://www.helpguide.org/articles/mental-health/emotional-intelligence-eq.htm

10 Critical Thinking Activities for Kids https://readingeggs.com/articles/2014-10-15-critical-thinking-activities-for-kids/

REFERENCES

A Leader's Framework for Decision Making https://hbr.org/2007/11/a-leaders-framework-for-decision-making

The Role of Emotional Intelligence in Conflict Resolution https://www.linkedin.com/pulse/role-emotional-intelligence-conflict-resolution-how-manage-gaur

Strategic Decision Making - A Case Study https://www.militarystrategymagazine.com/article/strategic-decision-making-a-case-study/

Why you need diversity of thought on your team https://www.capitalonecareers.com/why-you-need-diversity-of-thought-on-your-team

10 critical thinking exercises to improve your mind - Indeed https://uk.indeed.com/career-advice/career-development/critical-thinking-exercises

Media Literacy Guide: How to Detect Bias in News Media - FAIR https://fair.org/take-action-now/media-activism-kit/how-to-detect-bias-in-news-media/

Ethical Dilemma - Definition, How to Solve, and Examples https://corporatefinanceinstitute.com/resources/esg/ethical-dilemma/

Use of Reflective Journaling to Understand Decision ... https://www.ncbi.nlm.nih.gov/pmc/articles/PMC6426332/

4 ways to overcome cognitive overload in your students https://www.innerdrive.co.uk/blog/overcome-cognitive-overload/

How to prioritize tasks when everything feels important https://zapier.com/blog/how-to-prioritize/

To Learn Better, Make Mistakes | Psychology Today Canada https://www.psychologytoday.com/ca/blog/finding-new-home/202203/learn-better-make-mistakes

How to Be Open-Minded and Why It Matters https://www.verywellmind.com/be-more-open-minded-4690673

The Socratic Method: What It Is and How to Use It in Your ... https://www.goalcast.com/socratic-method/

CBT Techniques: 25 Cognitive Behavioral Therapy ... https://positivepsychology.com/cbt-cognitive-behavioral-therapy-techniques-worksheets/

Balancing Intuition and Rationality in Decision-Making https://www.meetelp.com/en/blog/balancing-intuition-and-rationality-in-decision-making

Self-development through reflective practice https://medium.com/@shilpa.ukau/self-development-through-reflective-practice-75cd36bbd2ff

Section 11. Building Inclusive Communities https://ctb.ku.edu/en/table-of-contents/culture/cultural-competence/inclusive-communities/main

Active Learning - Center for Educational Innovation https://cei.umn.edu/teaching-resources/active-learning

How to Design a Critical Thinking Workshop for Your Team https://www.linkedin.com/advice/3/how-can-you-design-workshop-improve-critical-thinking-u000e

Gamifying the development of critical thinking in education https://drimify.com/en/resources/gamifying-development-critical-thinking-education

Fostering Students' Creativity and Critical Thinking https://www.oecd.org/education/fostering-students-creativity-and-critical-thinking-62212c37-en.htm

7 Reasons Your Critical Thinking Skills are Vital to Democracy https://citizenos.com/news/7-reasons-your-critical-thinking-skills-are-vital-to-democracy/

Collaborative Intelligence: Humans and AI Are Joining Forces https://hbr.org/2018/07/collaborative-intelligence-humans-and-ai-are-joining-forces

7 Bona Fide Best Sites to Sharpen Critical Thinking Skills https://www.missiontolearn.com/sharpen-critical-thinking-skills/

Made in the USA
Columbia, SC
15 April 2025